WALKOFLIFE

Feet On The Ground

PAUL
NORTHRIDGE

WALK OF LIFE

Feet On The Ground

Walk Of Life - Feet On The Ground
By Paul Northridge

Published 2018 by Sazmick Books
Web: www.sazmickbooks.com

British Library Cataloguing-in Publication Data.
A catalogue record for this book is available from the British
Library.

ISBN: 978-1-912400-16-4

Printed and bound in the UK
using sustainable resources

DEDICATION

*This book is dedicated to my family and close friends
who have always been there for me; whether it was
to give me a kick up the bottom when I needed it or
their love when I also needed it. To Yulia, my wife and
soulmate - I believe soulmates exist because souls return
to learn more, and I believe that my wife and I knew
each other before this life – you're an amazing person,
the kindest soul, strong, humorous, extremely patient,
and I am so glad that you and I found each other. To my
parents and my brother, you all share the same qualities
as my wife, and I would like to say that I would not
be here now without all of your love and support, so I
am extremely grateful for you being you. Also, to our
daughter, Anya, thank you for choosing me to be your
Dad. I am so happy to see you become an intelligent,
funny, spontaneous young lady, and I am incredibly
excited to see what will happen in your future.*

Contents

INTRODUCTION

This is a book about me, Paul Northridge, but you've never heard of me, right? Just to give you some insights before we get to the whole story, I thought I should let you know that I have a low ego, so I don't think I will change the world, although I wish to contribute in the best way I can. I want to help people, and this is the basis of my book, which tells of my life up to now, at 43 years of age.

A word of warning is to not to drink alcohol while reading this book as I have written it at tangents, so it will leap from one subject to another, then return to a previous subject. It's also not the book for the light-hearted as it can get into some deep topics, but it does include a lot of humour to counter-balance.

I'm not going to say that this is a self-help book, as help is inside you and you must tune in to what you really need. I sometimes reflect on a great American comedian who said, "If you're looking for self-help, why would you read a book written by somebody else?'' This book is about the connection and learning stemming from my Near-Death Experience (NDE), which you will read about later. My wish is that my NDE will help people who are afraid of death. It's also about seeing my life as a disabled chap and the experiences relating to that. My life is a unique one. All life stories are unique, and it may inspire to write your own story. It's a book that will mention suicidal tendencies and an alcohol addiction battle. I hope this book will make you laugh, maybe shed a few tears, but really to realise that we are here together and to make our lives as happy as possible. My final goal is to get another few words into the dictionary, which you'll see throughout this book.

Chapter 1

Miracles or Magic?

Day one. I was born in 1972 in a normal maternity home, with normal parents, and with one normal brother who was one year and two months older than me. However, I, this new baby boy who had just popped out, was not so normal, and my life was never going to be normal but hey, what is normal? I born in the early hours on 16th April and nearly died straight after due to a loss of blood, which will be explained shortly. My parents did not have a clue as to what was going on because, as soon as I popped out from my mother's tummy, after we shared a few moments together, I had to be rushed for major surgery at a local hospital. During the 1970s, there were no scans to know if your baby was a boy or a girl – it was always a surprise – let alone to know if the baby was healthy or not.

I had a hole which was the size of a two pence piece in my lower back, and therefore lost a lot of blood. The doctors acted quickly and the hole was sewn up, but I could not return to my mother's arms as I had to get better in an incubator to help with breathing and to recover from the operation. My parents, Christine and Terry, were told that their son had Spina Bifida, which was a mysterious defect to them as they had never heard of it until that day. Whilst I was recovering, another problem started to happen; my head began to get bigger and bigger. This was not, unfortunately, due to my brain developing at a faster rate, but it was due to a fluid/water getting into my brain, called Hydrocephalus. This problem, again, was making me so poorly that I was on the brink of dying again. My doctors and parents had decided to go with another operation called a shunt. This was a risky operation which could potentially give me brain damage or I could die during the procedure. Both my parents and doctors had no other choice, as it was either try or die anyway.

My parents were completely upset, confused, and went through a whirlwind of emotions. The joy and excitement of having a son born into the world was knocked out with a punch of pain, unknowing, and helplessness. They had no other alternative but to agree to the risky operation, but they wanted to make sure that I was to be baptised first in order to give my name officially in case anything was to go wrong. This would give me the chance to be sent to Heaven if the worst was going to happen, as my Mum was Catholic.

The evening before the shunt operation was due, I was baptised, and all the family were there in the hospital. The nurses did a wonderful job by decorating the room with religious symbols, and it looked like the nearest thing to being in a real church. The priest blessed me and, as the holy water went over my large head, my parents thought something magical happened. It was a huge emotional event. However, it was difficult to get the priest there in the first place. The priest did not want to go to a hospital on an evening, as he was quite happy to stay at home with a glass or two of wine (as the rumour spread around our small town would tell you). Even after much persuasion was offered, it was still turned down. That was until my Nana decided to make a call to a Nun who she worked for at a Catholic school. This then snowballed, and so, eventually, the priest caved in. The priest was supplied with copious amounts of alcohol after the baptism, so all were happy in the end, especially as the news came from the local radio station that Derby County Football Club had won the league, so it was a double whammy for all that loved me and that loved the local football team. This memory was linked to my Dad, who's an avid football fan.

Driving back home with no option but to leave me in hospital, my parents were quiet in the car, exhausted completely from all the emotion, and tired from the sleepless nights of worry of losing me. However, they had one sentence of hope that my Dad said to my Mum; "I really hope that baptism works for him". Sure enough, as if by magic, a miracle, or perhaps just naturally, I started to improve overnight. The swelling in my head made such a significant improvement by the morning that the hospital staff notified the surgeon, who then cancelled the operation! My parents were ecstatic; who was to know if it was a miracle or some kind of magic that happened that evening? The truth was that I was getting better. Later in my life, I found out that this was called Arrested Hydrocephalus and it was common enough to give such a title of a condition. There is little known, though, with how the brain is affected with such a condition from my research. In my adult years, I wondered if it affects how I sometimes think or process things.

So, let me tell you a bit more about me. I was born with a defect by the full title of Spina Bifida Occulta. If you are unsure what it is, or you want to know more, let me tell you briefly about it. Spina Bifida can happen to anyone; in many cases, there are people out there who are walking around and not knowing that they have it. There are extreme levels of the condition, where you cannot walk at all and are paralysed from the neck down. It was rumoured in the 1970s that the chemicals sprayed on potatoes caused the defect, but later it was found not to be the case. There are cases where Hydrocephalus can cause brain damage. The less severe cases of Spina Bifida are where someone may never know they have it until they have an x-ray of their spine and then BINGO!!! I could give more information, but I think it would be better just to Google it, as there are so many levels of Spina Bifida. It's important to know the ways to prevent Spina Bifida in this day and age; there are things like folic acid, plus surgeons can actually operate prior to the baby's birth to heal up the hole in the spine.

I was a lucky baby. Lucky, you may question. That I had been at death's door twice in such a small period of my life?! Yes, lucky as I had amazing parents and a brother firstly, and you'll read later as to why I am saying such. I was not one of the lucky ones who find out in later life that I have the condition, as you know already. I was lucky because I can feel one half of my right leg and most of my left leg. There are some very unfortunate Spina Bifida people who are more severely paralysed or damaged terribly from Hydrocephalus. I was lucky that I had brilliant and genius surgeons and hospital staff. I was lucky that the brain swelling that happened did not cause too much damage, and I was lucky to be alive.

(My mum and I arriving home after recovering from Hydrocephalus.)

Once the immediate dangers were over, it came to the forefront that I had body issues. I could not feel my legs superbly well, and it was found that I had no right hip. This is where Mr Lunt came into my life, who was a genius, to say the least. He had the idea to use parts of my pelvis bone, which would grow back, and then sculpt the bone into the shape of a hip. This would give me the chance to have more movement if, and when, the time came for me to begin to walk. Furthermore, the hip would also grow like any normal bone and that meant it was not going to need changing in years to come. It was a huge success and it was the first time that I had to be in plaster, but it was the shape of things to come. The plaster was too big for such a tiny baby boy; it covered both legs with a pole in-between to keep the legs separated. However, it was now time for me to leave the hospital and to go home so I could be with my family.

(I'm in plaster following the hip operation.)

Ashley, my brother, had to spend most of his time at our grandparents', aunts' and uncles', due to the fact our parents were regularly visiting me in hospital. It was great to see his brother home, although I looked different to what he had expected, especially since my head was still rather large and I still looked ill. There were going to be moments to come where Ashley's life was not going to be the same, either.

After the new hip was in and healed, it meant that the plaster was removed. There were going to be more operations ahead, all to set up the foundations to get me on my feet in the next few years. I had thigh operations, feet operations, and more. It was a busy few years for me, my family, and the doctors. The hospital felt like a second home for me, as I spent a lot of time there rather than home. All of these operations were extremely successful and they were being done by a GENIUS of a surgeon, Mr Newton. He was an amazing man, a pioneer, and he would be the man who would get me on to my feet, technically speaking. My Dad was really concerned that his son may not walk, as he had no guarantee from anyone, until he bumped into a Paediatrician in the hospital that knew me. His answer motivated my Dad when he said, "Paul will walk, in his own unique way, but he won't make the football team!"

It wasn't until, aged two and a half, that I took my small but significant steps to walk. Like all children seeing their parents walk, I instinctively wanted to do the same. I grabbed on to the settee to pull myself up and began to walk whilst still holding on to it. My parents were, of course, thrilled by this wonderful vision. Later, my parents encouraged me to hold their hands so I could explore the downstairs part of the house. Eventually, I was walking by myself, with great relief from my parents and Mr Newton.

However, it was noticed that my right foot was floppy and that this was making it difficult to follow through with my leg, so back to the hospital I went. I could not feel my foot at all, and so Mr Newton thought it would be best to fuse the foot, thus being flat on the floor. Sure enough, I was able to walk with less of a chance of falling over. Eventually,

I was able to run even if it was only at a jogging pace.

Chapter 2

Keep Getting Back On My Feet

I was growing fast and getting to the age to start Primary School, but faced one more problem; I was not eating very well at all and I was sickly thin. It was the hospital food which I had taken a disliking to, and it had put me off eating. This was making me weak, and I was not ready for school. My parents tried to be crafty with my Yorkshire puddings as they knew I would eat them, so they'd insert pieces of meat to help me with getting protein. It worked for a little while, but then I found out what they were doing and took the pieces out. The next thing was to try me with the two-egg chocolate mousse which was approved by me, and I could not stop eating them. Yes, it was protein getting into my system, but it wasn't enough. The last resort was a conversation from Father to son, man versus young boy, and it was there that I was persuaded to experiment with food otherwise I would never get to school! From then on, I began to try new things. I was really keen on trying new things in life and school interested me, as I always saw my brother getting dressed in the morning in his school uniform and coming back home happy in the afternoon.

School time was great for me, also. I could draw, paint, and make friends. Furthermore, when the school bell rang for home time, my Mum was waiting with a chocolate bar in the car. Bonus! However, as time went by, the children began to become wise to my differences; I was not as fast as them at running, and I also started to develop a more noticeable limp which caused my constant headaches. This was due to my right leg not growing as fast as my left. Normal boots were not helping and, at that time, I could only wear baseball shoes. These baseball shoes were difficult for my Mum to get, as she had to buy different sizes due to my left foot being bigger than my right. Shop assistants were not at all able to supply half-pair of shoes, so my parents had to buy two pairs. It was time to get abnormal shoes, and this is when my heartache began to develop. I had to have a built-up shoe on my right foot, with a calliper up to the knee, and so, eventually, it was agreed that I could wear trousers all the time. Shorts were used especially in the summer time and, again, it drew the wrong kind of attention. These differences caught the eyes of all the children, as I went to a 'normal' school with 'normal' pupils, but I was anything but normal in the eyes of the children who went to a Catholic Primary School.

The bullying began when I wasn't able to play with other children at break times. When trying to be involved in the game of 'Tag', I was hardly ever 'It', even though I was not as fast as the others. I was also the last one chosen in any team sports. Not to mention, I didn't really converse with fellow pupils in class or at break times. I began to find comfort in playing on my own during breaks with a special Matchbox car which had flames all over the paintwork. It was my pride and joy, until one boy decided he liked it and took it off me. There was not a chance I could catch up to him to take it back, so I just sat on the steps leading to the school, tears welling up, and thinking about how I did not want to be in this school anymore. Later, I adapted what to play with as I had a calculator that played a numbers game. This was not attractive to those who could take it, so I was able to play still during breaks. This game also helped me to add numbers together and make up ten, so it helped my learning.

There were reasons that kept me there at school; my smiling Mum waiting in the car with that bar of chocolate after school, and my Nana Flo working in the school office. I would often go over to the office during breaks to have small chats with her, and she would also give me small treats.

I understood that I was different, but I really could not pinpoint as to why. In my mind, I could not see that I walked different and thought that everyone was having their operations during the summer breaks. My parents scheduled in the operations during the summer holiday as to avoid missing too much school time. Plus, I never saw myself walking in the mirror, camcorders were not around too much at that time, and I did not feel that I walked with a limp. I thought that these special shoes were something I would one day be without. I could not understand why I was different, and was made to be different by the other pupils in the school. I must say, sadly, that there were three boys especially that liked to make sure I was regularly reminded that I WAS different and not welcomed in their class. The three boys were each other's friends, and they would remind me of the way I walked by copying my gait, and by giving me names like 'Big Foot' due to my raised right boot. Eventually, I reached boiling point with hurtful words and with not being accepted in the school. The result ended up with a boy (not one of the trio of boys but another bully, nonetheless) and myself having a fight. Needless to say, children gathered around the event. It was me in the blue corner and other boy in the red. The scrap was mainly based on closed eyes, flying fists which hardly ever connected, and a lot of rolling around in the muddy hollow. On getting back up on to my feet again, there was one moment at the right time and angle where I was able to pick up my built-up right boot, which had two inches of wood inside. I pulled back my foot and – KICK – right onto the shin of the boy, who fell to the ground like a bag of potatoes. At that moment, children who had watched realised that I had a weapon if it came to a fight, but it still never deterred those three boys. If anything, it just made them work more as a team, which was harder to get than just with one on their own.

The worst part of the bullying, for me, was being brave to it all. Not showing the bullies or my classmates that I was upset in any way. It was like I wanted to show, 'you can keep giving it and it won't bother me'. Even my parents were not aware of what was going on until the day I could not carry the burden on my shoulders anymore. I broke down in uncontrollable tears and I painted a picture of how my life was unbearable in school, especially with those three boys. The main boy was known by my Dad, who then went to have words with this boy's Dad. It was not the way to handle things as it is now, as schools handle these things better, but it had to end. This intimidation had to stop. What was said between each of our Dads that night remains unknown, but it worked on that boy. However, the other boys still carried on. The bullying had lessened, although I was always going to be last chosen in teams and isolated throughout lunchtimes. At these moments, I was thinking that one day I would find a genie in a bottle who would grant me one wish only. That wish would not be that I would be rich, it would not to be popular at school, but it would be to make this walking issue just go away or just to be more involved with other pupils.

It was not just the children who made school time difficult, though. It was also my carer, as caring was not her speciality because she was an office lady who worked alongside my Nana. She was one of those women who you would think, in the first instance, that she was not a polite lady and just looked miserable, always. Even thought we are taught at an early age never to judge on appearances, on this occasion, your gut instinct would be correct. She would more than likely look happier if she chewed on wasps or walked on broken glass. She saw the world with grey-tinted spectacles. I think you get the idea. Anyway, she was chosen by someone who will remain anonymous to help me to dress before and after both swimming and P.E. lessons. She would be the one who'd help when I could not get to the toilet in time - that happened regularly - and she'd 'help' to get me cleaned up. Once cleaned, I had to wear paper pants and take a bag holding my dirty pants to give to my Mum. I had a choice; have the 'help' of being cleaned and risk the chance of being shouted at, pulled, and pushed by my helper, or risk the chance of being pushed and pulled by pupils and being name-called if they found out. Either way, it was going to be name-calling, pushed, pulled, and shouted at. It was not a situation that I looked forward to, and it was painful to attend school. Thus, not only was I nicknamed 'Big Foot', but it would also be 'Smelly Pants' which children would regularly remind me of.

I tried allsorts to avoid school; cold and cough acts, running into the bathroom to be 'sick', and trying to have a bad stomach before setting off. These tactics would sometimes work, but often they did not. This is when school became a chore for me. I would often go into my own dream world during school lessons, and float into a land which was more favourable. There were tooth fairies that I would talk to, clouds that I would shape into animals or people and then eat, along with animals that I could talk to and make more interesting topics of what they like to do when people are not watching them. The animals that I would daydream about would dance and sing and generally have parties all the time, which sounded great. I would also look around the school grounds in search of a diamond, which would make me both rich and popular! It also helped to take away the fact that I was not doing so well in school; I was not able to be in the same league as the others, which kept those three boys entertained in reminding me of how stupid I was. My parents did their best in keeping me up to date; they even hired private tuition where I learnt how to write artistically during one summer break between the red and blue lines. I was in plaster, as usual, when the teacher who they usually hired taught me how to do fractions and times tables but some of it did not sink in - let me rephrase that - MOST of it did not sink in. I got back into school around two or three weeks later and mimed the 6 times table when the class did it together, which the teacher failed to see. However, I was not so lucky to mime the recorder - the small woodwind instrument - as I got caught when I missed the crucial elements of where the notes were and then thrown out, which meant that I had to spend lunch times again on my own.

I had to come out early from school at times for doctor appointments, and so I was in my element there. The Children's Hospital was like home sweet home, so to speak, for me, and the Sister in charge of the appointments/waiting room knew me and my parents. She would give us a slight nod of the head to gesture to jump ahead of the queue and to sit in the second part to wait to see Mr Newton. It had its privileges, being regular visitors, although no, it was not really etiquette, or the British way, to queue jump. Needless to say, when it came to the time that I had to move on to more adult hospitals, both myself and my parents presented the Sister with cut-glass wine glasses as a token of all the help and care which she had shown over the years.

This is when it got to the worst part of the hospital visits at the Ronnie McKeith Centre, which I dreaded so much that my parents kept my appointments under wraps until the day itself. On arrival to the centre, it felt so much like how a dog in the vet could feel; being prodded, poked, weighed, and urine samples taken. In fact, most of this procedure was done with me being in just my underpants. Not only was it an invasion of privacy but the lady, like my school carer who did these chores on children, also loved to chew wasps. This lady did not give any reassurance to the lad in front of her and it was all done very clinically indeed. Once I was leaving the clinic, I would then hear her shriek "NEXT", which invited the poor unwilling victim. It was either that or to spend a few hours at school, but they were both as awkward as each other.

Ok, back to my own time and enjoyments as I don't want you to think that my life was all doom and gloom. It was quite the opposite, to be frank. I enjoyed so much time with my brother, Ashley, as we did things which I could do but would also give enjoyment to both of us. We would spend hours playing darts on the dartboard which hung on Ashley's bedroom door. Now, we knew the rules of the 501 game and it took a bit of time to get down to the doubles at the end of the game, but we got there. To be honest with you, we improved and were on occasions hitting the bullseye, even getting the occasional 180s, so that was brilliant. However, the trouble of hitting the doubles was not so good for Ashley's poor bedroom door. The door just looked like woodworm had a party. It had been filled and refilled so many times in attempts to repair it but it would just need replacing. My family and I loved to watch Bullseye for a Sunday television treat. It got to the point where our Dad got tickets to be a part of the audience where they recorded two shows in one evening. Jim Bowen would change his suit and tie mid-way and would tell jokes during the breaks. He was a bit blue, to say the least! It was awesome to be relatively close to a celebrity like Jim Bowen and there was even the bonus of seeing a professional dart player who played for the contestant's charity.

Another thing that Ashley and I would do was to play football against each other. It would mean that I would not be able to tackle Ashley so well but, when I was in the goal, it was more challenging to score against me. However, right next to the goals was a rose bush, which I would regularly forget about. At these moments of amnesia, I would end up in the rose bush, only to stop the ball from crossing past the line. This meant that I had regular thorns removed from my back and shoulders from my Mum.

(Ashley and I playing together or I am trying to run Ashley over!)

Home was lovely for me as it was a place of comfort. I had

my own bedroom where I would be for a lot of my time as I was comfortable to be on my own. The house was a place where my parents once married, moved into, and there they stayed. Home was like an olde worlde pub, with wooden beams across the ceiling and ornaments on every shelf. There were hundreds of Royal Jubilee cups and plates. There were also souvenirs from places they had visited and Royal Crown Derby plates, plus pictures on the walls from local artists which were increasing in price slowly but also looked lovely and were a talking piece to visitors. My parents gradually built their home by extending it, thus allowing their sons to have separate bedrooms. Ashley and I also played together in the local Miners Welfare Club on the pool table where Ashley was mainly the chap who won as he had a natural ability with sports.

Then there was my darker side, which I need to mention. It was maybe due to me being unhappy in school that I, during the warmer weather spells, wanted to dissect the daddy longlegs which I caught. I did the same to ladybirds and butterflies. Butterflies had the worst impact as, during one summer's day, I got out my tennis racket and proceeded to hit as many as possible. The garden eventually looked like confetti was sprawled all over. This period in my life also ended as shortly as it arrived, fortunately for the butterflies' sakes. I also had short moments in my life where I wanted to be the bully in school, as I wanted to give the same pain as I was feeling. It was like a catch-22 situation; I was in pain and wanted to give pain, but then I felt bad so I stopped doing it.

My school reports were pretty standard most of the time; 'He is a lovely boy and a pleasure to teach. I just wished he would spend less time daydreaming!' However, there was once, when I was nine years old, that the parents evening did not go my way. Whatever the teacher had told my Dad that evening wound him up like a coil, and my Dad was not best pleased. I had to hide at that moment until Mum had calmed the situation. It was clear that this teacher, which I hasten to add was unsure how to behave with a boy with a disability, could not adapt to seeing me uninvolved in many things. Or was it this teacher who did not want to get involved and was ignored most of the time? I don't want to say it was all bad; some of the teachers were amazingly kind, warm, funny and, of course, educational.

(Ashley and I on a school photo.)

However, this did not last long since it was a Catholic school, one of the more religious teachers thought she would be able to help me in getting better with my legs. She got her hands on some holy water and, most dinner times, I would attend prayers with splashing of holy water on my head and legs. This was confusing somewhat, as I still did not understand that I had a problem with my legs and thought that whatever had happened to me would be short-lived. I just thought that one day I would be just like my brother, but no matter how hard I prayed and asked God to make me better, nothing happened, which was getting rather disappointing. The Sister at the school took me to a spiritual healing church at one point. This was as scary as anything from a child's perspective as those from the audience queued up to be healed by the priest. I watched the healer ahead as he put his hand on each person's forehead and the next thing was that each person was collapsing on the floor or into people's hands behind them. When it got to my turn, I just found it nervously funny and the collapsing bit did not happen to me. This made me think that I did not get cured because I laughed at God and at the idea of miracles.

(Dad and I after my First Holy Communion at school.)

Although, there were still good things to overrule anything negative, I thought to myself. As the healers could not do anything, I still had faith, and that was in Mr Newton who operated on me twelve times. Every time I would have an operation I would be in plaster, and the children would love to doodle on the plaster so then I would be popular for this time. Being in a wheelchair meant that I was not walking, so no-one would make fun of me as the scary 'caring' lady would frighten them off!

The big day of the plaster to come off was one weird time. Firstly, it was chilling having a circular saw going up and down my leg. I was concerned that it would slice into the leg but that never happened amazingly, and to my relief. The plaster was then cracked open like an egg and what you get is one thin and white leg underneath. In my eyes, it looked like a new leg. The next port of call was to have the stitches out, which was so picky and sore. That, however, was my Dad's worst bit as I grabbed onto his hand for support. My Dad's huge hands blushed through many shades of reds, purples, and blues, but the best was yet to come. It was amazing to be carried out by my Dad on his enormous shoulders; I felt like I was ten feet tall, an absolute giant. If I was not allowed to be carried, then I was pushed in the wheelchair. Waiting at home was a huge, deep, hot bath made ready by Mum, where the itchiness of the stitches dissolved in the hot relaxation. I closed my eyes and beamed a wide smile; it was sheer luxury as the bubbles worked their magic.

Chapter 3

Screw Loose

Mr Newton was a genius. I know I've said it before but it will be something which will be mentioned throughout because without Mr Newton, I would not be on my two feet at all. Anyway, because of Mr Newton's geniusosity – I know that's not a word before you go delving into the dictionary and starting your letter of complaint, but I hope you can understand my meaning. Maybe it will become a word in the dictionary one day so please, spread the word! – yes, his geniusosity meant to me that Mr Newton was always looking to help. He was not afraid to experiment, and he had an amazing sense of humour. Mr Newton had a warm gleam in his eyes and a welcoming smile. He found ways in getting me to improve my walking and once, I found that my hip was going in the wrong direction, so a titanium plate was fitted to fix it into place. This was at the very same time when Barry Sheene, the famous British motorcyclist, fell off his bike and had his body full of plates. My Dad remarked often that I had the same, so I felt special and like I was a bit similar to this daredevil racer. This plate did the trick but one morning, I got of bed to go school and found a lump, right at the hip area. I said "Dad, please can you have a look at this!"

My Dad was concerned, of course, with this huge lump and got on the phone to speak to Mr Newton. Jokingly, Mr Newton replied, "It sounds like Paul has got a screw loose!" It was a funny remark for a surgeon to say as it suggested also that I was missing something in my brain too; maybe he was correct somewhat! He was right about the screw loose as the x-ray later showed, and the plate had to come out. I came out of the anaesthetic haze, after having the plate removed, and there it was right next to me on the cabinet like a trophy. It was my pride and joy which I kept in my drawer at home so that I could remember this event whenever I had a gloomy day.

Well, I don't want to go back to the lady at school who chewed wasps to help her to smile but needs must. Well, I need to tell you one thing about me, and that is that I could swim like a fish. Even though I could not walk very far or very fast, I could swim for miles. Once the carer had 'helped' me to change, I would have swimming lessons and then fifteen minutes of swimming fun was had by all. I would dive under the water for long periods of time to imagine swimming with fish and dolphins. I escaped from other children splashing each other at the surface and it felt like waves crashing above me. I earned the bronze medal in swimming too, which made me proud. I was recognised by my family for swimming so well, as they also loved to take me in the evenings and it was then that they decided I should swim for charity.

(This photo was taken during the charity swim.)

My Mum and I went around all the family and neighbours to ask them to sponsor me for The British Heart Foundation charity. I collected so much sponsorship money and was challenged to do thirty lengths of the pool. Surely enough, it was under the watchful eyes of my family – which made me proud – that I did it! Afterwards, I was challenged by the manager of the charity to do two more lengths and he would give £5 more to the charity. Even though I was tired, I could not resist the dare, so off I went again to prove that I could do it. The bonus for me was that I proved that I could swim so well in front of many but I was also later awarded with a certificate and a beautiful silver pen which went into my drawer, along with the titanium plate.

My drawer was built, over many years, of memories which helped to reflect on those times and to give me great feelings if the day ever got too much. There were stones that I found on the Torquay beach, there were shells from Skegness seaside. There were coins from my first trip to Spain, and badges from a trip to Jersey. There were bangles from when I stayed at the hospital that had my name, date of birth, and date of when the operation was. There was my first watch which had broken, but I could not throw it away. There were photos of me as a baby in an incubator. These were all amongst many, many more items that I loved and could not throw away. Where I would try out the Rubik's cube and the Rubik snake but after ten minutes of giving it a go it was a certainty that my brain was not designed for such puzzles. Yet it fascinated me to see how fast others could do it and wondered; how on earth are they doing that?

Scalextrics and Lego were also shared with my brother and I, plus it was a better waste of time than the Rubik's. I also could love the daredevil aspect of my life through my Evel Knievil action figure and machines of motorbikes and rockets. I would design ramps and circuits to give more of a challenge to the stunt doll jumping over my action men figures or Matchbox cars.

My life away from school was quite a simple one, really. I enjoyed collecting stamps which were First Day Covers, and I liked to examine my drawer of said many items. I enjoyed play fighting with my brother and we did, at times, get out of hand. Things got broken in the home but, with some super glue and the talents of Ashley, our parents weren't to know, until now! When the weekends arrived, it was great fun, with Friday nights at the local Miner's Welfare Club where I could play Bingo. It was here where I would find 'Legs Eleven' and 'Sixty-Nine' funny, and it was great to get the chance to win a little bit of money. Plus, there were things on offer in the evenings to go with my glass of shandy (beer and lemonade), as one keen gardener came in with bags of garden peas still in the pod, which were so lovely and sweet. Sometimes, a fishmonger came around with things like mussels in a container or king prawns with vinegar, which was delicious. Saturday mornings was Tiswas on the television, which meant mornings of mayhem with a young Chris Tarrant and Lenny Henry; it was crazy and so much fun! Sunday afternoons was to play Fives and Threes which was a domino game in the Miner's Welfare, or to play Running Out (another domino game) with Ashley, our Dad and Granddad Walter. I was actually getting crafty at knowing who had which dominoes by counting which ones had been played already. These games were played for money where both Ashley and I ended up with coppers (one/two pence) of about 50p each, which went into our piggy bank. These piggy banks were little safes that Ashley and I had where a special combination opened the door. We would often, on a Sunday evening, count how much we had and think of what to buy once we had saved enough.

Walter was my Dad's Dad. Walter was a big chap, like my Dad, both with huge shoulders, practical, and with clever minds. He was extremely supportive of his Grandson with sponsoring the swim for Heart Foundation, and even paid for a machine which would aim at improving circulation on the right paralysed leg. During the night my leg was cold, as paralysed legs are cold due to a lack of circulation. This machine was very expensive but it did a good job of keeping my leg warm. This machine, however, was the brunt of the C.Bs (walkie talkie truckers) as, whenever they got near my house, they lost signal to talk to their buddies. I also had a C.B which was a godsend to me, as it helped me to connect with people who I didn't know and to get to know them. I learned how to communicate this way, because this hardly happened to me at school. I did not know what to say and what to do but the C.B helped to build up my confidence. That was until I turned on the machine which circulated my blood!

Granddad Walter was also the one who got my main hobby underway, which was the electronic organ. I had tried the acoustic guitar, learnt within eight weeks the very basics of the back and the front parts of the guitar, learnt the names of the strings, and learnt note reading, but the lessons were repetitive and very little was learnt thereafter. The other instrument I tried was the recorder but, as you've already learnt, I had been thrown out of the class at school. One Christmas evening, I saw my cousin, Russ, playing the organ and that started my passion. It was amazing to see both hands and feet on the go and to basically be a one-man band.

From that moment on, I was addicted. I learnt the traditional tune 'Chopsticks' with my cousin, Russ, and then had a go with some of the typical Christmas tunes. There was no stopping me at that moment; it was music all the way. I had been given my first organ, called a Kawai, by both of my Granddads' help and that's where I met Mick, my first organ teacher. At this time, I learnt melodies, harmonies, and so many tunes. I also got to play between the games of Bingo at the Miner's Welfare, plus I got paid for it. Bonus!

(Told you I had a large organ!)

Luckily, I then heard of Tim Flint, who was a local concert organist, travelling throughout the UK and Europe. Tim shone like a diamond; from his beaming face to the rings on his fingers. He was the Liberace of the organ world. He was not only a great musician, but he entertained with comedy, had loud costume changes with sequins, and donned large rings on his fingers which were all musical emblems! Tim was great for me. He helped to get my playing skills up so much more and later, I would get to do music exams, concerts, amongst other things, which we will touch upon later.

A few years later, Granddad Walter died from cancer. It was my first experience of a loved one passing away. I understood that he was ill but not how extreme it was. I realised more later when he had lost so much weight, and he had such a horrid rattling (later called the 'death rattle') noise when he was breathing. The escalation of cancer was so fast that he had to be moved to the MacMillan ward, and there he stayed until he passed away. It happened over the Christmas period, and it made such a joyful time such a sad time. We thought we had lost him on Christmas day, but he stayed strong to pass away on Boxing Day. It was here that I kept my most treasured memory of Walter, and that was when we went fishing together. All I could catch was the tree behind me, and Granddad had to unravel the mess for me more times than he managed to actually fish.

I had still my Mum's parents around; my Nana, called Flo, who, as you may remember, worked at my Primary School and Ron, my Granddad, who retired early from British Rail due to ill health and was a really funny yet quiet but very intelligent guy. He was ex-military and had served in World War Two. There are a couple of quick stories to share with you about Ron.

The first one was that Terry (my Dad), when dating (my Mum) Christine, ruled the clock like an Army General. If Terry arrived late to take Christine home, Ron would rush out to the car and WHAM, he would whack the roof of Terry's car, state to him what time it was, and tell him that he disapproved of the relationship. Over time they grew to love each other, and Terry became the son that they never had, as Christine had a sister named Pamela but no brother.

Ron's second funny story begins with the fact that he liked to get people drunk, it amused him so much, and he also enjoyed having debates about anything and everything. He was funny in my eyes as I thought he was Eric Morecambe from Morecambe & Wise; he looked ever so similar to him. He had the similar humour, and he use to make me laugh by chasing me around the garden. Once, he left me in charge of the Sangria at one summer party and I was drunk for the very first time. It was slightly under the legal age, I am sorry to say, and I really don't encourage any underage drinking. The next thing that I remembered was being hosed down with cold water and supplied with cups of black coffee on the patio. Ron and my Dad would frequent parties that would not end until they had devoured a bottle of whisky that Ron had bought a few days before, not that it would be a problem for them both but, before that, they had shared wine and bitters to warm them up. Needless to say, the next morning both of them encountered pounding headaches. Ron had invited some nuns up for meals as his wife worked in my Catholic school. The evening would consist of usual deep conversation which Ron dwelled on, which hid the fact that, whilst the nuns were responding back, he would sneakily top up their wine glasses. If they saw what he was doing, they would only ask for a little top-up, where Ron's wrist would flinch and the wine bottle lowered more than it should, thus filling the glass more than they wished. It would be a shame to waste it, thought the nuns. The nuns came up the hill to their home for the start of the night and Ron would gladly see them roll back down at the end of it.

Chapter 4

Daredevil Paul Takes Early Retirement

Back to school again. I know, it's like marmite; you either loved it or hated it. In my case, I think you know by now which side of the fence I was on. I loathed it even more when it came to school sports days and the event of playing cricket. For an interesting fact, the school had real cricket balls to play with, which landed once on my head. Obviously I could not bowl nor could I bat, so the position of fielder was given to me. I was getting a bit bored during one game and was striking up a conversation with another fielder. Then, all I could hear were the words "Paul!" and "catch it" but, as I turned to look up, the ball whacked straight onto my forehead. This impact knocked me out instantly and gave a large bump on the forehead. I was revived on the field and took to the medical room to stay there for the rest of the afternoon. The nun teachers who handed me over to my Mum stated that Paul just fell over. Tut-tut, and the nuns say they follow the commandments! Even to this day I have a dent on my head, but it's covered by my hairline. The nuns thought it would be a good idea to still involve me in any sports by giving me head starts on the races and giving me the easier tasks, but I would still come in last. This did not go unnoticed and I was reminded again by the children. However, I was now ten and a new, bigger school was on the horizon with much bigger children, and therefore it may be a better time.

However, I must point out to you that I had a mate just up the street called Mark. He, too, had his problems with walking and so nothing was of an embarrassment to us. We knew that we both could not walk so well and it was never discussed; we only talked about what was on TV last night or we just played cards together, but the one thing we loved to do the most was to race each other. Mark had a tricycle and I had a scooter. I used to have a tricycle but my limited hip movement made it hard to get from A to B, plus I did fall off it once. The outcome of that accident was being rushed into hospital to have stitches in a cut above the left eye.

One summer's day, Mark and I were racing to and from both of our homes on the pavement, as there were not many folks walking, but we got carried away in the moment and I went further down the hill. This time I could not stop because the hill was too slanted and there were no brakes on the scooter as it was like a skateboard with handlebars. I knew that I was in trouble as a bend in the slope was in the foreground. Although, like a stunt rider, I took the corner well, I did not see the dip ahead, and I came off immediately.

I landed on the road in sheer agony, and it was a pain I had never experienced before. The pains of any operation or recovery were nothing to the pain I was feeling now. I could not move, and although Mark tried to help me up, it was impossible. There was only one variation; leave me where I was and Mark had to go to get my Mum. The wait felt like days whilst I wriggled in huge discomfort until Mum came in her car. We got home and I had a long hot bath to soothe the pain. Once I got out, I experienced another sensation; the feeling of fainting again. Remember the cricket ball incident? It just washed right over me and I could not do anything about it. Whoosh! Next thing I see is Mum over me trying to get me to come round.

My knee, by then, was three times bigger than it should have been, and very heavily bruised. There was only one thing to do, and that was to take me to the GP. My doctor saw my knee and thought it was just badly bruised. For four or maybe five days later of being in pure agony, it was time to have a second opinion. I was refusing to even try to walk. I went to hospital for it to be x-rayed, which concluded that I had not only broken my kneecap but that I suffered a torn ligament as well. Once again I was in plaster, and was to be in plaster throughout the first two weeks of attending my new school. However, before we get onto that subject, let me tell you that the very next day, that scooter went straight to the local skip yard. You see, it was not the first time I had fallen off it. I, the daredevil, had come off before and it was a bunny- hopping mistake which landed me with a fractured right ankle with another six weeks in plaster! It wasn't a surprise that that accident ended my daredevil career.

Let me tell you of some other bits and bobs about my Primary School life, which may be of interest to you.

Like I said before, I had very little understanding of my legs and the problems that came with them. If you'd asked me, aged 10, about it, you would get to know that I had already had so many more operations than any normal person who had lived a full life, but I had not had as many as other unfortunate children. I would say that operations were something that we all have to go through and that one day I would become like everyone else. I would say that I loved speed until the scooter-into-the-skip incident. I would say that I loved to play fight with my brother, and that I loved to watch TV, especially cartoons of Tom and Jerry or Sylvester and Tweety Pie, and to the extreme of Tiswas. Tiswas was so influential that I made Lenny Henry's condensed milk sandwiches - messy food indeed. I would say that I went to church with my family every Sunday, but I was getting a bit grumpy with religion by then. This grumpiness was due to the fact that the school nuns did not help very much... See their previous history of the aforementioned cricket ball and the splashing of holy water which did diddlysquat! Plus, the new priest in church was asking too many questions at confession time, and was not only bugging me, but my Mum too! I would say that I had tried sport as a hobby, as my Dad and brother both played golf together. However, in a comical way, I would swing at the ball, miss it completely, and end up with my arse on the grass. I tried to dabble in karate because I thought that I wanted to break things with my bare hands to scare off the bullies. The first and only karate lesson I had got too much for me when the class was looking at me as being 'different', so it was a quick dash outside where I cried non-stop for hours. But this didn't faze me, no way! My Mum's loving arms gave me all the comfort I needed, and her reassuring words would inspire me to think of the next thing.

I would tell you I loved to draw and was not too bad at it either. I would make birthday, Mother's/Father's Day, and anniversary cards all by hand with cartoon characters of my Mum and Dad. I would tell you I was a big fan of the magazine/comic called 'The Beano' but not 'The Dandy'. I would tell of the great things that had happened to me so far. I would remember watching Condorman with Mum in the cinema with the talented actor Michael Crawford. I also watched E.T in the cinema with my cousin, Russ, and on the way back I ate my first doner kebab. Boy, I really admired my cousin!

Holidays were amazing. We visited Spain and met two very funny and kind waiters who we had regular ten-pin competitions with. There was one holiday in Torquay that had family-run B&B where I got friendly with their daughter, but she looked more like a boy, so I was forever saying things like 'him' instead of 'her', which was both embarrassing and confusing. I would tell you about my visits to Alton Towers with Russ and getting both almost sick on the Pirate Ship and scared to death on the ghost ride. I would tell you about the time I went to Twycross Zoo with my Dad and we laughed out loud when we watched a younger chimp wind up his elders who wanted to sleep in the den. He peered inside of the den where they slept in, found an empty bread basket to toss inside the den, and then ran away as fast as possible. This did not get the desired reaction and, in fact, got no reaction at all. So off he crept again, but this time with a wooden box. He tossed it straight into the den and the next thing, all hell was let loose. The elders were doing their best to catch this fast younger chimp to tell him off, but it did not seem to work as he was too fast. I would tell you about the times I would spend with my Dad during summer breaks, travelling up and down the country as my Dad sold oil to many companies. We'd often get near to RAF bases and watch the planes either taking off or landing. We saw the large Vulcan fly right above our heads, which was an amazing sight. We travelled as far as Scotland and took a well-earned break at a roadside cafe for a bacon butty with stottie bread; highly recommendable!

I would tell you of one funny story where, during one summer break, I had yet another plaster which covered both legs, went right up to my waist, and had a bar across, similar to one I was put in when I had a new hip as a baby. However, this operation was to position that hip better and help me walk less like John Wayne in a cowboy movie. This meant that it was really difficult to get around, of course, so Ashley and I, whilst being looked after by our Nana, designed the idea of the wheelbarrow. Ashley took my feet and I would use my strong arms (by years of crutch usage, they were very powerful for a boy of eight!) to move my torso. Step-by-step, under Nana's supervision, we would make our way outside into the beautiful warm sun. However, something took over, which was my need for speed! I got faster as poor Ashley had the difficulty of trying to keep up whilst both of us were laughing so hard. This game did not last long as, suddenly, SPLAT, the wheelbarrow gave way. The plaster shattered onto the ground and Nana's face was an absolute picture of shock. It was just like 'The Scream' by Edvard Munch! Within a short period of time, Mum was home from work and had gotten an ambulance to arrive. My first experience of travelling in an ambulance (except my very first journey from maternity to hospital, but I can't remember that!) was short but great fun, with the siren wailing above me. The plaster was redone and there was to be no more moments of wheelbarrow madness.

I would tell you about how I got an amazing score on Lazer Quest on the Atari video game system, which had very simple graphics to that of the consoles of today. I played it for what seemed like hours and the score was deemed worthy enough to be photographed and sent to Atari. I would say about the time I went fishing with my dad where we once caught a swan by accident and the swan was not best pleased. It shows, with the swan incident and the fishing line into the tree incident, fishing was not my best sport! It was the same with being unleashed in the fairground dodgems where I was being my usual daredevil self, but we will swiftly gloss over the moment where I nearly shot the attendant of the tin can range.

Whenever I visited my grandparents', it was either going to be tiffin or choccy cake on the menu, made by Nana's skilful hands. I really was easily bribed to do anything if chocolate was involved, such as going to school. However, there was one thing that was nearly worse than school and that was the circus. The circus only gave me an adverse reaction to clowns and people dressing up as animals; one of which landed on mum's lap. I shoved him straight off... "and that will teach you".

I would also say that I had hope for my right paralysed leg, as I was able to get the big toe and the one next to it to move away from each other. It was found by coincidence when I went upside down on the settee and saw that, by flexing some muscle on my thigh area, I could make the toes move such like a chain reaction.

You see, I had these memories to fall back on at any given time and, like I said, it was not a world of doom and gloom. Plus, I did forget to mention that I had a few friends in Primary School. They weren't close but would talk to me yet I wasn't to be fully accepted in their group, so to speak.

Chapter 5

Chewing Wasps

Right then, let us get to the subject of my second school. So, just to recap, I had broken my knee and had torn a ligament, thus had two weeks left before the plaster was due to come off. It was extremely daunting seeing all these bigger children who could be perceived as young adults, and here came new blood into the school, like small fish for the sharks to prey on. Between that moment of coming out from the comfort of Dad's car and then having fifteen minutes before the bell rang to come inside was one mass of confusion. I checked that the main double doors were locked. Some older pupils said they open as soon as the school bell rang. There were no seats or benches to park my bottom anywhere. Then, all of a sudden, I saw two huge, stone, rectangular blocks near to the entrance where nobody was sitting and off I hobbled to sit down. These blocks became my area to sit all the time in the years to come during both breaks and lunches. The stone blocks were warm in the summer as the sun heated them up, but they weren't so nice in the bleak mid-winter! A longer coat was required to cover the rear end to avoid being stuck to it after thirty minutes of sitting.

The first morning of my first day at the new school came and went. Lunchtime came, and it was sandwiches made by Mum for me. I ate them sitting on these stone blocks. Afterwards, I decided to have a look around the premises. Slowly hobbling on my crutches, I saw the new tennis court, very nice, I thought, much more superior than the previous Primary School! Although, why should I be impressed really, because I had no intention of being in them? But within seconds, I was by hit a wall of people. It was overwhelming with all these young teens asking me questions about my legs and why I was born this way. The situation was too much and the tears just flooded out. Two young ladies dispersed the crowd and gave comfort to me. They told me of the last school assembly before the summer break where the headmaster advised pupils that a young lad with a disability was coming in September. They were told to make me feel welcomed, and to make me feel like I was normal. Well, that did not happen, as you may have gathered! It just got the inquisitive young minds even more so. These two young ladies were so kind and would often, at break times, sit with me. It was to be my first crush on a girl, but I was far too young for that kind of thing. However, it was this moment when the mass of children crowded around that I knew I was different. It was as if a switch had just clicked on in my brain and, from that moment on, things were going to be different in how I viewed life.

This new school with new surroundings still kept the old traditions as I was still bullied by new children and some old ones who had also transferred to this school, mores the pity. One boy thought it was a genius of an idea to call me a new name of 'CriPaul' as in as play on the word 'cripple'. This boy would often take my pocket money off me and make me buy things off him even though I did not want to. This boy took pleasure at any time in tormenting me. At one point, this boy even put a stone into a snowball which he threw right into my face, thus giving me a bloody nose. It was difficult to tell the teacher who pleaded with me to come clean and say who the culprit was, but saying such would make the boy attack me more in revenge for spilling the beans. No, it would make my life a bit better by keeping quiet. Summer events like tug of war gave a bully (from previous school) boy the good enough reason to chant abuse at me and called me 'Bigfoot' again. He also stated to me how useless I was in all sports whilst I was stuck there (in a tug of war match), holding the rope, and looking at this dope beside me. How I wanted to simply drop the rope and drop this lad by one quick blow to the chin. It would have gotten me into trouble but it would've given me a whole lot of pleasure. The cautious side of me decided to support the tug of war team but we still lost and this gave the lad more evidence of what a waste of space I was.

So, as you may gather, that time in Secondary School was not a pleasure either. The teachers were strict, and in particular, one assistant who was a helper for those children who needed additional support in the Maths department, which they called the remedial class. I had missed so much education at Primary School with the operations I had been through, and I needed that extra help with Maths. Let me give you a simple equation which I learned whilst there; the class plus the boy who loved to me 'CriPaul', divided by the other delinquents, multiplied by a mad woman teacher, equalled A LOT OF STRESS. This lady teacher, like the carer I had known all too well in Primary School, loved to chew wasps which gave her the crazy eyes, where she often shouted at me for no good reason. Anyway, I moved on from that class; more for the fact that I could never ever grasp algebra to knowing the times tables to knowing long division. In my mind, I was never going to use them, so they never sunk in. I came into the normal classes for Maths again but it was just to jump through the hoops. If I got it, then it would be a bonus.

The same went with subjects of History, Geography, any of the sciences, Religious Education, and French. I would be on my best concentration for English, Art, and Music only. The Art classes were with the brilliant Mr Archer; he was different to the rest of the teachers, laidback with the radio on in the background. It did not feel like a lesson in any shape or form. The classroom was like an art studio with Mr Archer's work proudly hung up on the walls, along with his students' work. I was hoping that one day my work would be up, and I did manage to get a few up! Mr

Archer showed us how to use pastels, oils, and pencils. I was proud of my pictures of the fruit bowl and self-portrait to the detail of my left hand drawn in pencil. Time would whizz by when I was drawing, although I was never going to sell millions like Van Gogh, neither was it my intention to cut off one of my ears as I needed that for music. Music lessons were ok, although the teacher looked like a prude, and she was a prude from how she came across. It was rumoured, though, that she used old curtains to make her dresses, which was a possible fact. The dull colouring of her dress matched her personality and her lessons. I wanted to learn so much in these lessons, but it was literally like trying to get blood from a stone. The theme was mainly on classical music, which sent half the class to sleep while the other half looked awake but had drifted off in their own worlds. Then, the practical side of things began and that was more like it. There were bits on how to compose and dissect music, and this interested me more so. I was thinking that maybe one day I would write my own 'War of the Worlds' and make millions.

I was lucky during Physical Education, P.E for short, for most of the time I just stayed in the foyer of the school and read my books. Then later, I was asked to play table tennis with a young school lady. I could not move half as well as this young lady and yet I still won, so I questioned her. This is where she whispered, 'I was told to let you win by the teachers'. I said, 'come on, let's have a proper game', and from then onwards, it was more of a challenge for us both.

Sorry, I went a bit off-course there for many paragraphs! My plaster had come off for my broken left knee but there was a glitch, the knee would not straighten. This would be a major problem for anyone, but even more so for me, as the left leg was the strongest out of the two and helped so much with walking. This began another quest to get the knee straightened. Mr Newton tried with two operations; both of these were thought to be successful at the time, as the leg looked lovely and straight in the plaster. It looked the same without the plaster, also. But as time went by, the knee went back to the shape of how it was, even with so much painful physiotherapy and occupational therapy. I worked for endless hours on the exercise bike, where my Dad would be my coach to push me so much further than I could bear, yet my Mum would be there with loving arms to comfort me in the worst of times. It was asked by my parents if it was possible to have another go, maybe it would be third time lucky, but Mr Newton was unusually reluctant and advised it could lead to me having a permanently straight leg. Not being able to bend the knee was going to make life hard with stairs and driving when the time came. It was agreed by all that it was to stay how it was; bent, but at least functional. Another fact that I forgot mention was that whilst I was in hospital, I was winning the hearts of the nurses in the ward. Not only was I a lovely young lad, always smiling and easy going, but I always had strawberries on the cabinet next to me. These strawberries came from my Mum, who dipped them in melted chocolate which was then set in the fridge. Strawberries like this were like magnets for the nurses and a big pleasure for me to have. My parents knew that I was not very good with hospital food and they always came to visit me with something; even bringing bacon and mushroom sandwiches wrapped up in foil, which were the best on the planet. My parents were, by then, experts in visiting hospitals and knowing exactly what I loved.

I must mention one more humorous event that I can recall. I can't remember which operation it was, but I was recovering well a day or so afterwards, so Mr Newton did his usual rounds to see my recovery. He said things like, 'you're doing so well, maybe in a day or so we'll get you home' but my young ears heard, 'you're doing well' and 'home', so I called my parents on the hospital payphone. I told my parents to come and collect me. An hour or so later, my parents came to collect me and packed me up, but then the Sister in charge said that it was not possible for me to go yet. However, with a bit of the Northridge persuasion and my Mum's nursing skills, we got the go ahead to leave. Since that incident, Mr Newton called my parents 'The Escape Committee'.

During the years of Secondary School, it was apparent in my mind that I was going to do music all the way into my adulthood. From listening to it compulsively to Top of the Pops, music was so addictive; Thursday night was my TOTP night. I was confused to see such artists on television like Boy George performing 'Karma Chameleon', and trying to work out if I was seeing a man or a woman. It was music that I completely loved, from all eras, such as Belinda Carlisle, Roy Orbison, The Who, Wham, to even pub sing-a-long music which I played in the local Miner's Welfare on the organ. I was very eclectic as my parents loved Elvis Presley and Abba which rubbed off on me, but one band I could never grasp was The Beatles. Again, it was the marmite thing for me. How could anyone like 'Yellow Submarine'? That was my question. But it was Aha, the band from Norway which was popular in the late 80s that attracted me, and I envisioned being like the keyboard player in that band. I understood, from earwigging on girls' conversations, how gorgeous that keyboard player was from Aha. Maybe one day I could be admired that much?

My family and I travelled to see organists play throughout the country, and it was amazing to see the mechanics of it all; arms going ten to the dozen and feet dancing away, looking like Fred Astaire at moments. I was possibly thinking about one day being up on that very stage and performing in front of hundreds or thousands. It was daunting to perform to so many but possible, or so I thought. Once, when I watched my teacher, Tim Flint, in concert, it was amazing, as he had an overhead camera projection which added to the amazement of seeing those fingers burdened with heavy diamond encrusted rings going so rapidly. But, as mentioned before, Tim's humour shone so much that he had an aura which sparkled like his diamonds. I sat at the front with my parents and we managed to have packets of peanuts to share to nibble on whilst the music was blaring out. However, Tim's hearing was much more supreme to hear the rattling of the mentioned packet that my Dad tried to open it discretely. Tim ceased playing all of a sudden, turned around quickly to the point of the sound, and saw who it was. Tim came right off the stage and towards my family to grab the packet out of my Dad's hands and threw them on to the stage. Tim took a leisurely walk back on to the stage with hurls of laughter from the audience, made his way to the microphone and simply said, once the laughter died down, "Let that be a lesson to you all", as he pointed to the audience like a teacher to the naughty classroom. Again, and uproar of laughter came from the audience.

Also in the Secondary School years, I hit puberty. Things changed and grew as normal, and so did my feelings to the opposite sex. But there was an obstacle to tackle, and it was one huge obstacle; it was my legs, and how it made me different to the rest. From the moment of that switch going on in my head, which was mentioned on the first day of Secondary School, my views had changed. There was one young lady in many of my classes who I could not stop watching. This young lady was beautiful and radiated the whole classroom in my eyes, even to the extent that I ignored completely what was said in Geography, Science and History, and so on. I was too embarrassed to begin to make conversation with her, though. During the lessons, our eyes would meet and I instantly turned away with shy desperation. It was a confusing time for me as I was wondering whether she was feeling the same or whether she was possibly disgusted at the sight of me. I had never shown my feelings and now being aware of how I looked was not encouraging me. It was like I was a good looking young lad facially but otherwise a monster. Well, that's how I saw it anyway. I often thought I would do well in a P.T. Barnum type of circus, right next to the Elephant Man.

It was Valentine's Day and I was this twelve year old boy, so I thought to try something new. I wrote a card in different handwriting, snuck into the classroom during break-time, put the card into this young lady's bag, and then came out from the room as if nothing had happened. The bell rang to gather the classes and I sat in view whilst the girl looked into her bag for her textbooks, only to produce the card on top. My face began to feel the heat with embarrassment. She immediately opened the envelope to see the card and looked across only at me, so I turned away. Did she like it? I wondered to myself. What was going to happen next was a mystery to me. It was at the next moment that, again, changed everything, as it was assembly hall singing lessons. It was the worst thing for boys going through puberty to try to sing, especially whilst their voices were changing from soprano to tenor. These moments sounded exactly like a natural squeaky saxophone with a broken reed coming through the boys voices. What added to their dismay was that the girls sounded like angels and when the boys came in with their parts, it went quiet with awkwardness, except for some boys giving it a go with the teacher's forceful encouragement. Sorry for the slight deviation there for the moment. It just so happened that I was sat on a chair as I had no other choice even during school assembly, whilst the other pupils sat on the floor. Right in front of me was this young lady eagerly trying to get my attention. It was never going to happen as the hymn book was my shield, which came in very handy to hide my red face from her questions. The glances from the girl in the classes afterwards were laser beams of anger, rejection, and possibly hatred. I could no longer look at her in the same way as was the same, possibly, for her. Eventually she got a boyfriend, and it was rubbed into my face as they were a pair of love birds who could never be separated.

Love birds seemed to be catching on, as there were new couples sprouting out all over the place, or so it seemed to me. Even the school parties and discos in the evening showed it more so with those dancing in couples. These school parties were just a place for me to hit rock bottom. I sat on the chair all evening with very few people coming over to have a chat with me but to be an object of desire for the opposite sex seemed on the contrary, plus the question was, could I dance and would I want to anyway? My hopes from the start of every school party got slowly squashed in the excruciating two hours. To rub it further into my nose, the last dance of the evening was a slow, smooching ballad to give the boys a chance to go and ask a girl to dance. These types of parties grew even more love sick couples around the school. By the third school party, I had enough and declined any further invites to go, much to my parents' confusion and dismay. I was not the type to open my heart out all the time to my parents as I did not want to get them depressed so, most of the time, I was the strong and silent type of lad.

To distract me from all connection of romance was my evenings of pleasure of watching TV with seeing such stunners on Top of the Pops like Madonna showing off her bra, Olivia Newton John in the video of 'You're the One That I Want' in tight fitting leggings. When I was watching a film, I could just maybe get a glimpse of a bit more flesh like in 'Splash' with Daryl Hannah. I took comfort in chocolate, and my Mum's chocolate cake was something special to indulge in. There were never shortages of chocolate in the house and my waistline began to increase. Dad also regularly bought a huge box of mixed broken biscuits and they were amazing, but they vanished oh so quickly. Friday night was the treat of a Chinese take-away and my favourite was sweet and sour ribs where I needed a whole box of tissues to wipe the thick sauce off my hands or onto my shirt by accident. One Saturday, whilst heading off to watch sheep dog trials in Buxton (as my Dad was brought up as a farmer), we stopped off at a Little Chef. I had a full English breakfast with a chocolate milkshake. Now, the breakfast was ok, when you have the comparison of my parents' bacon and mushroom sandwiches with toasted-on-one-side bread.

The Little Chef breakfast was okay with bacon, eggs, and the rest of the trimmings, but the chocolate shake was out of this world. It was thick, rich, and so very chocolatey. It was at that very moment of seeing my eyes in sheer luxury that Dad persuaded the manager to buy a box of these shakes, and so the belt around my trousers moved up another notch.

Another way of avoiding hurtful emotions (sub-consciously) about the fairer sex was to play at home on the organ. Now, the puns about playing with my organ may fly at this stage, but they have all been heard so many times by now. I would study the TV listings as it consisted of only four channels at that time. It is to the contrary of this current generation where you can watch as much as you want, when you want, and if you can't find it there, it can found via the internet. Once I picked out a few programmes that all the family could also enjoy, I would then get the earphones plugged into the organ and off I practiced for a good few hours. Not to say I did a few hours every night - that would be incorrect - but I did work hard and the rewards were paying off. I was getting into the realms of more awkward pieces of music; one of which was called 'Blaze Away'. This was the pain in Ashley's side. Sometimes, and for such a long period of time, especially during half-term, the headphones would come off, the volume would be set to level ten, and I would blast out 'Blaze Away'. There was no escaping this. Even the comfort of Ashley's bedroom was not safe as the music would resonate, seeping through the walls. They would shake and the bass would pound against Ashley's bedroom door, asking to let the music in. The music would start, stop, start, and then stop again as I was making mistakes, but practice makes perfect, and off I tried once more. This led to moments of brotherly spats, but nothing was ever so severe to separate us, of course.

Chapter 6

Brilliant Betty

As brothers go, Ashley and I were different but shared the common link of love and respect for each other. Ashley had his friends both at school and outside of school. Ashley and I very rarely met until it was evenings together as a family at the dinner table. We shared the holidays as a family, doing things we loved to do together, and that always came back to play fighting. Now, I must add to this that sometimes it got a bit heated in the scraps we had. If, by any chance, accidentally, I need to add, either of us hit the Holy Grail of the man's worst area of where to get hit, then we were in trouble. Do I need to spell it out? Ok then, right between the legs; I don't need to go into much more detail than that, do I? Oh my goodness! Once that connection from the knee hit the crown jewels, the play fight turned to a real fight, where only exhaustion would end the battle or an apology would simply do. There was grappling, as usual, when the fight began, where Ashley and I were in some kind of body lock, and only Ashley's head could move. Ashley's head did move whilst my chin was directly above at that very moment. Within seconds of agony for both parties as we wiggled on the floor, Ashley was clutching the top of his head, I was grasping at my mouth. We eventually calmed down to find that I had a chipped a front tooth and that a small part of the tooth was embedded into Ashley's head. After this episode, the fighting got less and less, plus it was more controlled. At least there'll always be a part of me in Ashley's head.

Ashley was somewhat of a role model for me. He was everything that I was not in my mind, as Ashley could dance and play any sport with Dad, from golf to squash, where I would only be a spectator. I wanted so much to be like him, and I was quite simply in awe of my sibling. I even styled my hair in the same way, much to my brother's dismay. I watched how my brother would stand at the mirror, styling his hair, only to get a stuck-out tongue to state without words, 'oi, stop watching, will you?' But we also shared an interest in the early teenage years of weightlifting. Mainly, this was due to our cousin, Russell, who did the same. At one Christmas, I was presented with a set of weights, and there I would lift, either by myself, or spar with my brother. This helped so much for me to use crutches, and I had built up rather large shoulders which, out of everything negative about my body, I was kind of proud of. One little fact, at Secondary School I was the target, not to be bullied, but to try to beat at arm wrestling. This phase stopped when I had seen the sport of arm wrestling on television, after thinking that maybe I would take it up as a career. The visions I saw of men breaking their wrists whilst going against more muscular guys at arm wrestling put an end to that idea. But it was Arnold Schwarzenegger that I was inspired by at that time; I wanted to improve my upper body to that look so much that I trained most evenings. I knew still that I would not become that perfect to be in films, but that was not my aim.

Most siblings would put away any differences to help each other in times of crisis, and that was exactly how Ashley and I were together. Ashley had to put up with so much at times, as I was the focus of attention when I had operations and recovery. It must have been both difficult and emotional for Ashley at those times. We, as brothers, were good together, but sometimes competitive. In our teenage years, we would compete on how many bacon and mushroom sandwich towers we could devour. I remembered one amazing fact of my brother, when we were in a restaurant. Ashley ate a sixteen ounce steak within minutes and Dad challenged him to eat another. He put a one pound coin in front of Ashley and the challenge got underway. Amazingly, the second steak and chips vanished, and the pound coin vanished faster than the steak. Ashley was like a magician, I thought, truly amazing.

Our Dad did motivate Ashley and I by money. For example, he placed a ten pound note on the sideboard unit and stated that if, by the age of sixteen, we did not have a cigarette then those notes would be ours. Surely enough, that worked for us both, as there were many opportunities to join the other teenagers behind the bike sheds to give it a go, but I was strong as I wanted to make sure I would have that money. I was easily trained by money, or bribed, whichever way you see things. At least I was not addicted to smoking into adulthood.

During the years of Secondary School, again, I had made some connections to other classmates and some had taken me under their wings, but there were no real strong friendships, unfortunately. They would not miss me if I did not come over at break times, and the conversations were not really interested in what I had to say; it was somewhat superficial. It would be the concrete block near to reception where I was mainly steered towards, and I would sit and watch other classmates play with each other. I would watch different football matches over the long field in front of me, or another variation was to do homework which gave me free time in the evenings to read a book. The interesting magazine for most young lads at that time was called MAD. It was funny, weird, and totally different to the Beano which I grew out of.

I also had a keen interest in cooking, but it was frowned upon by the lads in school as it was seen as ladies who did all the cooking at that era. There were ladies like Delia Smith in the limelight of cookery TV, and no-one like Gordon Ramsey or Jamie Oliver at that time. I kept that interest to myself but, as I did not know how to tie my apron, the strings got neatly tucked into my trousers instead. Doing such meant to check that no-one watched and that my back was near to the wall. In cooking, I brought back home freshly made pizza and cakes. The scotch eggs did not make it to the plate as it looked like a dog had thrown up; sorry if you're reading this on your lunch at this point.

Another little story to share was during one autumn half-term break and it was decided, as a family, to visit the Major Oak in the Sherwood Forest. It was renowned for being the place where Robin Hood lived in the forest and hid in the Major Oak to avoid capture by the King's men. So I, with my family, parked up and I, using wooden 'up-to-the-armpit' type crutches at the time, hobbled to this huge tree. It was quite a distance travelling on foot and there were plenty of uneven paths, so it was difficult to go by crutches but, after about twenty minutes later, we made it there with the tree in all its glory. It was a huge tree, indeed, wider than any others that I had seen before. I imagined that Robin Hood was able to go into the tree's cave when the King's men were near. It was propped up, like scaffolding, to give the old tree a bit of support, and next to it was a plaque. This plaque gave the history of it all and reading on, it did mention that if Robin Hood existed in the 13th Century then the tree would have been a baby one and not at all able to hide Robin. My family and I were gobsmacked from this trip. I was extremely tired and in pain from the crutches digging under my armpits and into my shoulders. This is when my Dad came to the rescue, with his six-foot-four stature, placing me on top of his huge shoulders and off we went back to the car park. All our family would say in the car was these two words, "rip off!" My mum also had to nurse my hand blisters afterwards from the rubbing of the bars of the crutches, and that's what I had to remember the trip by.

One book gave me a great deal of pleasure and I could associate very well with it. It was called 'Adrian Mole's Diaries'. It was a series of books which told of how a nerdy young teenager tried to make his way into adulthood, with plenty of incidents along the way. It made humorous reading, and was slightly naughty but highly entertaining. I could simply lose myself in the break times at school. It kind of helped me to think that I was not the only one who was without a girlfriend in the teenage years and had a fixation of breasts! Along with a huge male population, I hasten to add. It was also the myth of sex at this time in my life. Just what was SEX? The sex education in classes really was aimed at the fact that a man and a woman can make babies with their different organs but that was it, unless I drifted off somewhere during the lecture. At this time of learning of the birds and the bees, it was an obvious thing not to do 'IT' at the time as AIDs came into the main focus with posters everywhere, so even if I wanted to know more about sex, it was something to keep me away. This is where I began writing my own diaries, like Adrian Mole, to say of my own experiences and feelings but to read them later became very embarrassing, enough to burn them, as I snuck them discretely under the pile of wood at a local bonfire night and made sure I stayed there until the discriminating pages had been burned to death along with poor Guy Fawkes.

So with the two knee operations (I hope I am not jumping around too much and if you are having a few glasses of wine whilst reading, it must be so much confusion!) not being all that successful, it was my left foot getting the brunt of this new style of walking. I was walking tiptoed on my left foot and eventually, a huge bunion grew just above the big toe. It was not just that, but it was also an in-growing big toenail which was giving me difficulties to walk plus a lot of pain, so another operation was underway for them to be sorted out. After the operation I thought to myself, what had I done? It was more pain than any of my operations. Whilst resting with another plaster in the middle of the night, all I would feel was a huge throbbing sensation on my foot keeping me awake. Besides, the bunion came back larger than life within months of it being removed, which brought attention to fellow children, not only in school but also outside of school in anywhere like shops or the cinema, and this was also to attract unwanted attention throughout my life. I now had two large boots to wear; one for the bunion on the left foot and one for the difference of length for the right leg. It was not my intention to give the bunion removal another go; I was not bothered about pain too much but that was another level up.

During my recovery from each operation, I had a lovely lady called Betty who did not at all need the assistance of wasps to help her to smile. The only problem was that I was grumpy now as a young teenager with my past experiences of carers. I had to be pushed around the north school to the south school in the wheelchair which I had on loan. Yet, I was fiercely independent and resented communication with this poor lady. Betty realised my grumpiness and even bought me presents on my birthday to calm the situation but it just re-ignited the fire even more so. I was so adamant to be in control of my wheelchair but I didn't see the dangers of if it tipped over. There are many regrets that I live with and that is one of them. I realised the errors of my ways and learnt how to treat people better in future.

Teenage years spurted my growth and the issue of leg lengths came into view so much more. The fact was that my right leg was not growing half as fast as the left, thus meaning that my right boot had to be built up more than usual, by four inches in total. This made it difficult to walk with, as the boot was bulky and heavy to swing through, even though it was made from cork. But it was thought in this time that I could perhaps manage without the calliper on the right leg and yes, it was freedom for me, as I was able to put my shoes on. The orthotist also took away the idea of shoelaces, and I was able to use Velcro straps to tighten up my boots, although I never learnt how to tie bows or knots, linking us back to the story of tying my apron during cooking lessons. It was especially brilliant that the orthotist was working in Wellingborough which meant days away from school to get them done. Later, the chance came to have them made locally, but the opportunity to miss school for that reason was good enough for me to travel with my Dad with wrapped up warm bacon sandwiches along the way. Gordon the shoemaker was a lovely chap with a big heart, who was passionate about his job, and the shoes were made to perfection. You could not make shoes with an invisibility shield sadly, but at least they fitted and were comfortable.

Chapter 7

Back From The Dead

One evening, when my family and I sat on the sofas at home, a TV programme called QED came on, which did documentaries if you have never heard of it before. This particular episode was filmed in Russia, where a surgeon was helping children with polio to stretch their leg bones with a device called the Verona Fixator. This gave my parents the incentive to ask Mr Newton about it. Mr Newton advised that he would research it and then come back to my parents. Oh, I forgot to mention to you that, on my last knee operation, Mr Newton stopped the growth spurt of the leg, but there was still that four inch difference. Hey, at least my left leg would not grow any more now.

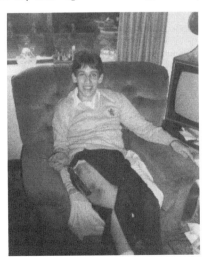

(This is the Verona fixator on the side of my right thigh.)

Weeks passed and then my parents had a call from Mr Newton's secretary, telling them to make an appointment at the hospital. This was interesting, because it was introduced to my parents that it was not just any appointment but it was to be a lecture where I would be on show in front of many other doctors and medical staff. The time came and I was without my trousers in front of about thirty people, some of which were quite attractive ladies on the front row, I thought to myself, and I was wearing only pants! At least these pants were clean and didn't have superhero characters on the front, phew. Mr Newton kicked off the lecture with me beside him on a hospital bed. It was explained how the procedure was new and that it had never been performed in the United Kingdom before or on a Spina Bifida lad. It was further explained that they were to cut my thigh from top to bottom, break the bone, insert two pins above the break, and two more below the break. All this talk was very daunting for both me and my parents, but all the operations prior to this were also nail-biting stuff as any operation had its risks but this meant either take a risk or live with the built-up boot. To hear 'break the leg bone'... Aaargh!

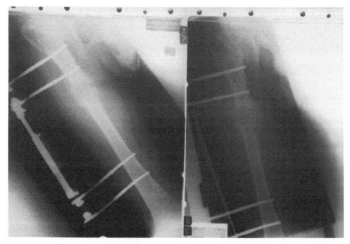

(Here's an x-ray of the Verona and the bone break has callous forming around trying to heal.)

I, along with my parents, made our way to the hospital and to ward eleven of the Derbyshire Royal Infirmary. It was all adults in the ward and here was me, aged fourteen. The first night was very peculiar as I could not sleep too well because I was thinking of the operation in the morning. Plus, it was 'Nil by Mouth' on the headboard, and I was thinking about food. Boy, I would do anything indeed for a bacon and mushroom sarnie. When I finally managed to get to sleep, I heard whispering noises next to me from the nurse's commotion. It was the man next to my bed who had unfortunately passed away. The curtains went around him and I could see no more than the bed being taken away with the sheets over the body. That night was a long, long night and I turned on my nightlight to do word searches to occupy my mind.

The morning came exceedingly slow for me. I was so tired that just maybe anaesthetic would not be needed at this time, I thought to myself. Also, I was in dire need to eat and, by now, three bacon sarnies would have been just the ticket. However, I was whizzed off to the preparation room. I had a heart monitor attached and was then given pre-meds to make me sleepy. It actually made me feel a little drunk as I stated my undying love to the nurse who looked after me, which made her giggle. I thought I was onto a winner; I was making her laugh and trying my best for her telephone number. Annoyingly, I was dragged away from my future wife/nurse into the operating theatre and was given a muscle relaxant and then the anaesthetic. However, I started to feel very strange indeed with a sensation that whooshed over me. I looked at my hands; they were bigger than usual and red. I brought this to Mr Newton's attention and the next thing I knew, it was black, as if someone had just turned me off like a television. With what felt instantaneously afterwards, I saw myself from above my body, as if I was floating near the ceiling. I could see all the staff, along with Mr Newton, rushing around to revive me. They moved all the operating gadgets away and started to give me things to bring me back.

It was like a dream and completely surreal to see myself below on the hospital bed with Mr Newton and his staff all around me, all of them working hard to bring me back to life. In this moment though, I knew it was me below somehow and I was ok with it. I felt tranquil. It kind of felt like a person looking at his car on fire but realising that it was only a material item. My body was the car; it was only my way of transport through that life. Soon after seeing myself on the bed with the staff attempting to resuscitate me, I was greeted by beings who gave out so much warmth and love. It was difficult to describe how they looked, but it was not people that I knew. It was almost as if the beings were glowing with pure light, transparent, caring, and true. I would say they looked almost like the typical tall grey alien, but with an aura around them. They encouraged me to come away from seeing this shocking vision of myself dying, and I floated away from there. I didn't even float away; I just arrived at another realm when I agreed to come away.

I was then given a lesson, or a life review, of what had happened, to experience the pains of which I had caused in the past. It was not forced onto me, but it was an agreement that I should look at my life experience thus far. I saw myself being the bully at school and how it confused and upset those I took it out on. I began to understand why, and that was due to the fact that I was being bullied myself and needed to feel powerful at that time of my life. I saw things in the future and how to look after myself, like how to behave with others. All of these emotions of pleasure and pain were also experienced by me, and I discovered how others felt at the time. However, there was no judgement of what happened when the painful lessons were taught; it was just something to learn about how to treat others better for the future.

I was able to see inside the body, to see how things we both do and eat affect the internal organs. It was an insight into what to eat and what not to. It was almost saying things like to be aware of fast food, as it will attack the heart. The same went with reproduction, as I saw how life came to be.

Oh, I forgot to mention that before the life review thing started, I could be anywhere in that moment. I saw my parents in their kitchen, preparing food, and that memory stayed with me to this very day, as I felt their excitement to see me later after my operation. They were looking forward to seeing my face when they presented me with their fabulous homemade food.

I had visions of future events that I had not experienced before, like driving a car. I felt the excitement of driving! I can remember being in another house where I had feelings of being miserable and depressed. I experienced the emotion of depression where I had nowhere else to go but to commit suicide. Strangely enough, I saw many death experiences of other suicides and even one where it was set in Roman times, or maybe Ancient Greece, where I died on a bed of spikes. I saw another death where I was stabbed in my car by someone I knew, yet felt their shock and confusion of asking themselves, what did I just do? I saw myself dying elderly in Russia with my family at my bedside. I saw another where I crashed my vehicle into a truck. Are these past experiences, my future, or different possibilities/roads to travel? I am not too sure to this day.

I saw how certain animals are and how they behave. I saw cats pulsating colours at their owners when they purr to show how much they love them and how much they enjoy being stroked. I saw dogs being completely different where they have a programme of being protectors of their owners and giving out unconditional love. I saw the energy of trees like it was bringing in an energy to be able to create a huge energy back out. It was almost like a blood circulation reaching up the trunk, to the branches, but seen in light and in bright colours.

I saw games being played by different souls. Games like Tag and another tennis type of game looked like lots of fun, but I did not have the opportunity to join in. They were getting their energy back; at least this was what I was feeling from them, or I was getting that information fed to me. At the same time, I was shown places where souls go for recuperation from a stressful previous life, almost in solitude as not to be disturbed but, again, I felt like I could see they were having colours as a type of therapy.

The life review was a whole lot of visions and too much to take in at once or to remember for later. Maybe it was due to my age or level of consciousness that I was not able to absorb it all. Following on from the life review, I was being asked about staying where I was or going back. I felt that it was not my time to stay in this beautiful place and that it would upset my family if I died. There was an urge not from me, but from somewhere else, stating that I had not done what I needed to do yet and therefore I had to return. It (the strong energy or maybe my own consciousness) was strongly indicated to me that I would go back anyway to learn the things which I needed to. During this moment there was this light, almost like a tunnel, which attracted me to go towards but knowing it would mean I would not come back as me. Maybe I did go through the tunnel, but it was hard to recollect. The next thing that I remembered was waking up in the hospital bed.

That was one crazy dream, I thought to myself, and with some aspect of truth. I felt so amazing as soon as the anaesthetic had worn off; maybe it was the adrenaline which I was given to bring me back to life. However, I felt well and when my family visited, it was great to see me in such high spirits. I had not looked at the thing on my leg but it weighed quite a lot and pulled at my skin. When my Dad pulled back the bedsheets to see the four pins sticking out from my leg, it was just the ticket to make Ashley almost keel over. It was a truly gruesome sight; the pins coming out from my thigh was unusual, and it had a black plastic and metal tube across it. This plastic tube was the part that would stretch the thigh with a special key. Mr Newton came around at the same time as my parents were there in the evening and I asked about the situation of my hands swelling up. Mr Newton explained to my family and I that I had nearly died, as I had an allergic reaction to the muscle relaxant medicine given but that they had managed to bring me back. So, perhaps what I saw was real, and maybe it was not a dream after all. It was not until years later that I saw a documentary of Near Death Experiences, where I found out I was not alone with sharing the same occurrence. I learned that some see loved ones who came to collect them when they died, but I could not say it was anyone I had met, such as my Granddad Walter who had passed away a year before. Some people stated that they saw God, but I did not encounter that as I also had a religious background but was, by this age, disgruntled by believing in such. Yet, many describe the feeling of pure calm, the life review, the tunnel with the light, and the choice to stay or go back.

This experience was a life-changer in how I perceived things. I had no real interest in religion anymore, and I was more for following on the way of how to be. I do not wish to be anti-religious, by the way; it was my own experience, and I feel that it's a free world to believe in what you want. The only thing that I wish is that religious people do not have an agenda, like to make money; "God told me to buy a large/fast plane, so I can spread the word". That, to me, is taking people's hard-working money. Another problem is that they will do many bad things only to confess on Sunday, so they'll feel better. I did not see that as a good way to be either. The actions of one person can affect others so very much for the future.

I naturally felt that reincarnation was something that could be chosen when death occurs, or that we can choose to live in the other world. Later in my life, I have the feeling that we are all one consciousness, and that living our own reality is one aspect of that experience. But I felt that being on Earth was a learning experience, a school if that's ok to say, and that it was the goal of the soul to keep on developing. It is a bit deep, but it was important to explain to you how the experience changed my perception on life and death. I felt that when someone around me that I loved would die, yes there is a grieving process for the ones who are left behind, but I realised that they have gone to a lovely place and can come back again but in another body. To be honest, to die is to return to where you also belong. It's beautiful, it's pure love, and I have no fear to die. Death was not the end; that was my viewpoint. In fact, I had a small insight into reincarnation at about five years old when the news of Elvis Presley's death shocked so many people. I was having a bath whilst talking to my Mum about this subject. I said that maybe I could be Elvis, but just using another body. I then realised that Elvis had just died, so it was not possible for him to come straight into my body. It was difficult to explain it from a five year-old to an adult, but I knew what I meant and remembered the conversation very well with my Mum. Death was now, and throughout my adult life, something which was not concerning me in any shape or form. Maybe the body that we have is just a car and the life paths are just roads that we travel on... Deep, huh? And you thought you were reading about a young lad with a great sense of humour and not a deep thinker? Just one other thing that I also took from this event was that we choose our body. Yes, including myself taking on this challenge of being disabled. I chose to do it and to learn the events that I am learning still. It got a certain footballer into trouble for saying a similar thing, but I would like to support his viewpoint as it's very true. I feel it is also true that we have soul connections; in other words, a soul makes an agreement with another to reconnect with each other during this life so that they can learn certain things. It's like the feelings of, I know this person yet I have never met them before and yet we connect so well that maybe we have known each other in a previous life. It's a shame that we forget these agreements but if we did know, then it would probably reduce the learning. Although, saying that, there have been instances of children remembering their previous lives and giving so much detail that it makes it for certain in my eyes that reincarnation does happen.

Days passed by after the Verona was put in, and Dad was then able to turn the key on the new device on Boxing Day. Since it was Boxing Day, it kind of reminded the family of losing Granddad Walter, but this occasion of the Verona turned things to a positive. It was such a strange sensation of the bones being separated, only by a millimetre per day, but it was something which was indescribable. It was slightly painful and achy, but also created a pushing sensation inside my leg which felt like a centimetre push rather than a millimetre. My Mum's job was to regularly clean the skin around where the pins came out with iodine. This was not out of pleasure, as she had to pick off the dry old skin. Sorry, readers, I hope you're not passing out at this very moment. My mum used iodine to clean the area which created a very sharp pain but died away quickly. However, as it was a daily experience, it became tiring somewhat. I pleaded with my Mum for one day of rest from this pain, but it was not something that could be acceptable. I knew that it was going to be more painful if the open holes got infected, so I kept that in my mind.

On my return to school after the Christmas break, I became like a celebrity entering the school, but for the right reasons this time. The children were in awe, sickened, gobsmacked, curious, and just utterly amazed with what they saw. I was in the wheelchair again with cut-out trousers and this thing sticking out from my leg. It was just amazing to see for the children. I felt like a hero who has gone through this. Bring on the bullies to see what this lad is like, huh?

The time that the fixator was on my leg whizzed by and, two inches of growth later, it was apparent to my Dad that the top two pins were bending. This was explained, after having an x-ray by Mr Newton, that the callus which mends broken bones is getting harder and therefore unable to stretch this break any more. This was a little disappointing for my family and I as we were hoping for all four inches of growth. However, on reflection, it would have meant a larger thigh bone than my left leg, meaning my knees would not have aligned with each other.

An appointment came through the post to have the device removed and the day arrived quickly, which was a school day, bonus. My parents and I were taken to a cubicle within the Derbyshire Royal Infirmary. I was surrounded by the cubicle curtains and we listened out for Mr Newton getting nearer, patient by patient. Soon, Mr Newton arrived, smiling as usual, and advised us to get ready to have it removed now. I was in shock; what about preparation? Won't it mean an operation, or at least a local anaesthetic? But, to my dismay, Mr Newton proceeded to take the whole thing off! Now, the plastic tube was not a problem, but when it came to the four pins which really were long screws... It was a dull, achy pain as the screws made their way out from the bone, but then through the muscles to the fleshy part of the thigh was really painful. I decided to keep a brave face about it all and helped by keeping the swabs in place for any blood coming out. Believe it or not, there was not an awful amount of blood. I was expecting to see a lot more. Within about ten minutes, the ordeal was over and I could see four holes looking somewhat like bullet wounds. Another amazing fact was that the very next day, the holes were no longer there. The skin had closed and I was able to bathe properly. I really missed having a shower; that and also the privacy of it being on my own, not with my parents' supervision, was fantastic. However, my parents always did what they could. For example, when I had a plaster they got bin liners and sealed them tightly around them to prevent water getting in. Mum also found the longest knitting needle she could so that when I had an annoying itch half-way down my leg covered in plaster, out came this magic needle to reach the parts that other needles could not reach.

The problem with all of these operations was that I had to be a totally different person. To surrender my independence and have others around to help me to wash, get me anything I needed, and being pushed around from A to B. To have a bottle at the bedside to pee into, to be helped with the other thing than to pee (hopefully you understand other bodily functions). Not only was it annoying for me, but it was strenuous for my parents, of course. When I could not do much and wanted to keep my mind occupied, I did all sorts of things like crosswords, and playing both games of solitaire; the board game and the packet of cards type. Solitaire was quite apt for the games I played as I was mainly solitaire myself . The fixator was off my leg, healing nicely, and I was trying to get back on my feet. Weeks before it was due to be removed, my Dad knew some friends who loaned him scaffolding. It was erected outside just from the back door in the style of a treadmill where I could hold onto the sides of the scaffold poles. Slowly and surely, my legs were getting stronger everyday as I marched up and down for as long as possible in the wintry weather. So, with all of these experiences, I had grown up fast and was mature for my age. It was like I was in my twenties in my mind but in a teenager's body. That's not really a terrible fact; it's just that I struggled then to understand other kids' immaturity, and that happened into my adulthood too.

My Dad came up with wonderful ways of getting me on my legs, thinking outside of the box in many ways. Really, my Dad was a great thinker and wanted so much to get his son's feet on the ground. He had ideas of a sling which would hold metal weights and that would go over the left knee. With the leg stretched out, my foot on a stool, and the weights pushing the knee down, it may stretch the damaged tendon. I could put this sling on myself and often I would sit to watch television whilst the weights stretched the knee. This did work whilst I sat but, sadly, when standing up, the knee reverted back to being convex. My Dad, along with Granddad Walter a few years ago, bought an exercise bike where I would cycle as much as possible with altered pedals so the right hip with less movement would allow me still to pedal with the right foot. More often than not, the right foot would annoyingly come off the pedal, thus not allowing me to go faster than I wanted and, being a speed freak, this frustrated me so much. If it wasn't my foot coming off, it was the trouser leg getting stuck on the crank. Grrrrr! However, I could watch the TV to make the chore of cycling enjoyable, or put on the headphones to listen to Orson Wells' "War of the Worlds". I would lose myself in the musical story rather than the sweat and the pedalling.

My last, and fourteenth, operation by the age of 16 years old was the second attempt of the left knee straightening, and not long after that operation, Mr Newton deservedly retired. It was understood, though, that Mr Newton carried on doing many things like building canal boats and making boilers as he could do wonderful things with his hands and mind. He was a truly wonderful man. Stepping into this man's shoes was his understudy who was another very talented surgeon but sadly, it was my last operation with Mr Newton and the last operation that I was going to have, well, up to now anyway. I had many private consultations with this new consultant and others, but the truth was that I could walk, stand with poor balance, and tackle the stairs. The risks of any more operations could lead to losing it all. In many people's eyes, it was the truth, yet I did not want to hear. I was really up for the risks, but it takes two to tango. If a consultant did not want the risks, then who would? It meant really that I was stuck. It meant a life of not being 'normal' as it was plainly obvious that I had problems with walking. It was the smaller built-up boot of two inches, yet still there for all to see. The other boot was larger due to the huge bunion which refused to go away. I struggled to move the right hip, especially with a flexed left knee. No matter where I would go, I would draw unwanted attention. It was a particularly bad day if I was seen by a group of young children in the shop who would laugh at me, or just could not take their eyes off me. It was like seeing a car accident... Horrible to see and yet engrossing at the same time. It was often a case where children who had just started to talk and ask questions about everything they saw would see me and ask their Mummy as to 'why does that man walk so funny?' The poor Mum, with embarrassment, would either tell off the child by saying 'shut up', or some would just say 'not all can walk like you', which was a nice variation. I was disturbed to see myself in a reflection of a shop window or in a home video. My body image is disgusting, in my mind. I had never seen myself walking before, until the teenage years. It was this time when reality really hit; I was disabled, and nothing could be done about it. It was also a question, to me, of using crutches or a wheelchair. This would make things so difficult in shops when carrying stuff, so what was the point of having these operations to make me walk?!

I even had tried other avenues as my Uncle, Roy, was a faith healer. Now, at this age I was losing my religion and was unsure of whether to attend to this effort. I understood, from discussing it with my parents, that Roy was not based on a religion, so to speak, so I thought why not. I came into my Aunty and Uncle's home with my parents and began making conversation with my Aunty and then suddenly, a man came into the room. He looked like my Uncle but different, which was difficult to pinpoint, apart from his eyes looked in a state of a trance. He would then lay his hands over my legs without touching. He would mumble words which seemed another language like African, and his hands would shake vigorously. At this time, an enormous amount of heat omitted from his hands and my legs would stay so hot for hours after the visit that they would glow red like I had a suntan. I had about half a dozen trips to my uncle until the realisation dawned on them that the condition was too severe to help. Even still, my Uncle

Roy had helped so many with different circumstances or afflictions, and he described it as if someone took over his body at this time, like some kind of spirit.

My Dad had another idea of seeing a hypnotherapist for my knee to straighten it. I met the therapist and was brought into the study room where there was a couch to relax on. I listened to the relaxing music and her voice but that was it, nothing more. I did not go into any trance and really, I felt like I wanted to release a toxic gas from my rear end which was in my main focus to refrain from letting out. So I could not really relax, and the left leg did not straighten much at all. Maybe the leg was not possibly able to straighten by the mind as it was a damaged ligament. I was given tapes to listen to at home to practice this relaxation whilst focusing on a dot on the ceiling, but I still could not relax the muscle when I was walking.

Anyway, I tried, again, to keep my mind busy. If I had bad days, I would eat too much chocolate and my weight fluctuated. Besides that, I was busy both in school and after school, especially with another religious ceremony to prepare for, and that was Confirmation. This was to basically show that, as a young adult, I knew most of the religious stories and meanings behind them. This meant that, on a weekly basis, I would meet in a group with other teenagers going through the same process. The leader of the group would read stories from the gospel and asked questions to the group. The next thing to do was to choose a saint's name and do research on it. This saint's name would become my middle name but not really, as it was not on my birth certificate. I thought it was a pointless exercise, as this weekly meeting just threw me further away from religion and God. I was thinking that if God had made me as such, then he had a sick sense of humour. When that question was asked to religious people, they replied that God made me like that for a reason and one day I was to find out. This answer was not sinking into my mind as to what purpose it served. I then thought, was I being punished for something that I had done in a previous life? That made more sense. Or to go one stage further, maybe I had an old soul and I had chosen to come into this body to learn more?

Chapter 8

Dido and Aeneas

Many things occupied my teenage mind and that helped me to avoid concentrating on the truth. It was thoughts going around in my head about what life would be like in ten years from now. I thought I would be married with two children, just like how my parents had done. It's not like it was mentioned in any form from my parents, and it was just that which inspired me to become like them. It's like instinct to talk, walk, and fit in with the crowd; at that time it seemed that family was the norm, If a child came from a 'broken family' it was seen as different, yet today, it is possibly unusual to be in a 2.4 family, or is it?

The most strenuous time for me was when I needed to work on my GCSE exams. My mock exams were showing that I was not going to get brilliant results. I did miss a lot of time in school with hospital visits, and therefore it was possible that I would not do so well in the real GCSEs. It also did not help that my class year were like guinea pigs, as it was the first time GCSEs were introduced, and most teachers struggled with the curriculum which showed through a lot of pupils. I had grades that were not failures, but they were not in the areas of passing either, such as an A or B grade. After these results it was decision time; to either go to college or sixth form. For no reason at all that I can remember, I decided to stay at school that bit longer. It was a good year, as most of the bullying individuals had had enough of school and it was only the ones who wanted to work who stayed on. But remember the girl who I gave my first Valentine's card to? Well, she stayed on also and

I always saw her and her boyfriend hand-in-hand, which rubbed my nose in it all the time. Plus, I thought to myself that the lad she was with was a muppet. I wondered why she had chosen him, as if it was to annoy me more so, it had worked! It was a time that was pleasurable to be at school, however, to no longer be in uniform and to be the eldest of the whole school, apart from the teachers, of course. But maybe it was the teachers' style, maybe the teachers themselves who I found it hard to connect with, or maybe I did not try hard enough. Either way, my GCSEs were not passed that year again, which was gravely disappointing for both me and my parents. So, during the six weeks of the summer holidays, it was discussed and decided that it was time to try out new things, and that was to be South East Derbyshire College. Another new thing that was happening for me in that time was that I wanted to drive. My brother had been driving already and I was in awe when I sat next to him in the car. Ashley had an old Mini which he had converted with bucket seats to give it a low-to-the-ground feeling. Ashley was like Nigel Mansell in his day, and it was scary to be in the car with him but, with age, it altered somewhat. The challenge for me would be to get in and out of the car. I would kneel on the floor and then crawl in, doing the opposite to get out. One lesson for me at that time was not to buy a Mini when I pass my driving test.

Now, if a disabled person wanted to be on the roads, then it meant that they had to go through tests. I had tests of my reflexes, decision-making, and mental ability. This meant that I had to use a car simulator, and it was my quick reactions to emergency stops and alike which deemed I was able to be on the road. My provisional licence came through and I began to have lessons. I must point out to you that the ability tests perceived it that I should only drive hand-controlled cars. To seventeen-year-old me who still had awkwardness in accepting my disability, being in a hand-controlled car permanently would knock my confidence. When my driving instructor met me for the first lesson -

and this was a guy that had many years of training disabled drivers - he thought that hand controls were not right for me. So I began to drive just an ordinary automatic car. I could use my left foot for the accelerator and brake with no problem at all. By around about ten lessons, my parents and I thought it was time for me to have my own car to practice in. The car that we bought together was a white Vauxhall Astra Sport. It was a lovely car to drive, and had the speed when it was needed. Both Mum and Dad gave me lessons between my usual ones. The lessons with my parents got a bit fraught, as most teenagers with parents do.

The driving instructor used to make me laugh whilst driving, which was not the best thing as my eyes closed for a few valuable seconds. From telling me that the no overtaking sign was ok if you had a red Mini, to asking why cat's eyes are bumpy. It's for the visually impaired to tell them they are too close to the next lane. These jokes had to be done at the right time and that was in the stop position. The driving instructor thought that I was now ready to put in for my test. In October that year, and still being seventeen, amazingly I passed on my first attempt, even though the test itself did not go how either I, or the examiner, wanted. The examiner could not find a clear corner for me to reverse around so I avoided that manoeuvre, much to my relief, as that was my weakest point. I stammered my answers out on the Highway Code tests, but I still passed. I was overjoyed, and it marked the day of freedom for me.

I say freedom because I could ride a modified bicycle but I could not walk very far, so I always relied on my parents to taxi me everywhere. There was no stopping me from going anywhere I wanted to go in my little Astra. It was somewhat scary driving on my own for the first time and without someone next to me to give me instructions. Yet, in time, driving became second nature for me and a real passion in my life. I loved that Astra car so much that I gave it the name of 'Super Duper'; only because the car registration looked alike and matched to my feelings. I always loved music, and cranked up the volume as I drove. The same things happened back in my bedroom with the hi-fi blurting out and then Ashley in his bedroom doing exactly the same. Looking back, all I can say is sorry to our parents!

Anyway, back to no more school and hello to a new life in college. My first day there was unexpected, completely. I knew that my brother went there and that Ashley loved it, but it was not to say that it was going to be the same for me. There were all kinds of characters at this place. There were the rockers with their long hair, dressed in their favourite band t-shirts and ripped jeans. There were the goths, who dressed all in black, and who had white powered faces and delicately done eye make-up with cobweb designs. I thought to myself, at what crazy hour are they waking up just to be ready for college? Then there were the other students, who demonstrated that they wanted to be on their own, for example, one man who wore no shoes, whatever the weather. He also wore a trilby hat, long doctor's white jacket, and sported long hair and a beard. It was very hippy-looking but with an edge of the Manson family. No-one would dare talk to him and I think it was somewhat scary to the teachers also. Plus there were people like me, normal, well at least dressed normally... The jeans and a t-shirt type of a guy.

My first lesson on the first day of college was music; great. This is where I met my first two friends that would be for life. Now, I was unsure where to sit as the classroom did not have any tables to begin with, it was in rows of chairs. The back rows were all pretty much taken, leaving the front rows with free seats. Next to me was a guy much older than I was, and who I was not sure of whether to make a connection with. I wasn't a person who wanted to judge, as I did not like being judged, but I went with my gut feeling a lot. On the other side was a young chap who introduced himself as Lee. We hit it off very well as we were both playing keyboard instruments; I had the organ and Lee had his piano. During the interval, Lee and I discussed music and, overhearing just behind us, was a chap called Dave. He was another fellow organist, so all three chaps stuck together through one main connection of music.

Throughout the times there, Lee got bored to say the least. He was a natural entertainer and to sit during hours of musical history was not what he had signed up for. He thought it was going to be more practical learning, like how to learn the piano more. To say true, it was not his cup of tea, either, to know composers' dates of how long they lived on earth for, and it was pretty much mind-numbing. Plus, one music teacher dissected operas and concertos of the Renaissance period. It sent half the class to sleep, and the only thing that Lee and I picked up on was what a Tierce De Picardie was. That will give you something to research! Lee also changed the words of a title of an opera called Dido and Aeneas by composer Henry Purcel. Lee's variation of this opera title was something to do with sex toys and the bottom area, if you get my meaning! The teacher was so engrossed in this era of music, and you could see how it was wonderful that maybe she wanted to live in this time by the clothes she was in but, to the class, it was to jump through these loops to get the qualifications to then become a musician, and that was my goal too.

The practical side of things was superb. There was a young teacher called Greg. He had long, pony-tailed, ginger hair and a wicked sense of humour. The class learnt the basics of a recording studio. One exciting moment in my life was when I wrote lyrics, which Greg showed me how to form chords to them and within a few hours of jamming, plus recording, the song came to life in the studio. The cassette recording of 'What Do I Have to Do?' was regularly played on the journey back home, blasting out on my player. The class remarked how good it was and that maybe it would be a career for me. It was just a coincidence that Kylie

Minogue had a hit song a few years later with the same title.

There was one lovely teacher called Tony who also played the organ and had a passion for symphonies and would blast them out. I am sure the art class next door would hear it also, yet it would aid their creativeness. When the music would get to the more relaxing movements, Tony's eyes lowered, and the class would see that he was sound asleep. The class thought, just maybe they'd be able to leave the class after it had finished if he was still asleep but somehow, he would come out from his trance, wide awake, to ask questions about the piece. Most of the class were distracted by this plot to leave early, that they missed those moments they'd be asked questions on. He also introduced humour into music by showing extreme music pieces by John Cage which did not have any music at all. It was silence for over three minutes and the world going by was the music... Wow! By the way, I am being sarcastic. Then there was Dudley Moore, a very talented gentleman as an actor and musician, where he would create Colonel Bogey March with the never-ending cadence. This is where the listener thinks the music is coming to an end, but then the artist would go off at another tangent, and that happens for another five minutes. Have a listen if you get the chance, as it is funny indeed.

I loved the mixture of music and comedy where there were moments of greatness. Things such as Morecambe and Wise when they invited the conductor Andrei Preview, sorry, I meant to say Previn. Then there's Weird Al Yankovic taking popular songs and changing the lyrics to make them funny. Then there are the films of Charlie Chaplin set to music. Comedy and music worked hand-in-hand with one another. That was just to name but a few things which are worth finding out about. Oh, and not forgetting Tom and Jerry cartoons, which were awesome with animation and music.

There was a practical teacher who helped me to improve playing the organ. Kevin was a young teacher at college and he was an amazing player. Kevin taught with great passion and the lessons were never dull. He would try to explain difficult rhythms to me with humorous concepts, which were highly entertaining. The fact was that, with Kevin's help in college and Tim's help for private lessons at home, I passed London College of Music Grade 5 on the organ. The year after that, I would then pass Grade 8, which was the highest grade to pass. After Grade 8, it would be a diploma and then a degree, but I never chased after them.

Unfortunately, Lee, one of my new-found friends, decided to leave college as he had received an offer to entertain at a caravan holiday site in Mablethorpe, not too far from Skegness. However, we swapped contact details and would keep in touch. I wasn't going to forget about the moments of genius from Lee which gave me brilliant memories. Memories like when the class were in awe during a practical day of showing hidden talents because Lee pulled out his ukulele. He impersonated George Formby to perfection and, later, we were to be told he was a member of the George Formby Society. Lee would also show other songs that he knew from Kevin Bloody Wilson who was rude but so funny.

So Dave and I hung around college, and it was a time when I did not feel isolated anymore. I did not get bullied in any shape or form and did not seem to catch anyone's attention for all the wrong reasons. It was the best moments of my life. I had found friends, learning about something that I wanted to do, which was music, and thinking that what would happen in the future was anyone's guess. I wasn't sure what I wanted to do exactly, but becoming a performer was a possibility. The taste of playing in front of an audience was not daunting to me; sure, I got nervous behind the stage but once I was playing, the adrenaline took over. The possibility of becoming a music teacher was interesting, but I was not sure if I was in the realms of being as clever as my teachers. Maybe I would be a keyboard player in a band? In the few years at college, I had four

GCSE passes and two A-Levels. Although Maths was still a mystery to me as I still got a grade E for the third time, so I gave up Maths forever! It was this place of college where I broke away from school and the terrible connection associated with it, to becoming a young man with dreams.

My own, and Dave's, great taste in music showed me the way. I developed a love of the Rock-y side of music so much more. Dave helped me to explore Deep Purple, with 'Child in Time' being my favourite, as the organ music was the main solo. Iron Maiden was the next influence that I was steered towards, and it was fantastic, especially 'Hallowed Be Thy Name'. I bought all of the Iron Maiden albums, which were on vinyl at that time, and I recorded them onto cassette to listen to whilst driving, although it did not help with my speed as the loud music gave adrenaline to any young lad. Then, a band called Dogs D'amour came into sight which gave another angle of Rock with interesting topics. The reason for going into this line of music, for me, was again to escape the feelings of not being in love. Most of the heavy metal industry focused on being out of love or doing too much drinking. That summed up Dogs D'amour, along with the historical facts from Iron Maiden, with songs of 'The Flight of Icarus' and 'Rhyme of Ancient Mariner'. It was at that period of time that an older generation took a dislike to such types of music, stating that devil words can be heard when playing the songs backwards on the record player. However, it was not in my mind. I was impressed by the powerful vocals of Bruce Dickinson and that Bruce was both a pilot and a fencer so, in other words, a highly clever guy with a great voice. Plus, Deacon Blue and The Beautiful South albums were in my car when I wanted to be a bit more chilled out.

Dave and I spent a lot of time together, and most of that was meeting at a local restaurant of which we knew the managers very well. Best of all, the staff there were so very friendly; needless to say, I had a crush on one of the bar staff ladies and Dave had the same with a waitress, so they were good enough reasons to attend this establishment. Also, for the record, the steaks there were amazing, as the chefs cooked it to perfection, especially the chargrilled rib-eye steaks and proper chips cooked in dripping. This combination created fireworks in my mouth; it was food perfection. It would happen from time to time that the restaurant would get sold, and it would feel different with different management and food. However, Dave would keep his ear to the ground to hear that the managers who we liked and followed bought a new place, and then it would be the next place for the lads to pop over to. Because the staff knew us well, the bar staff use to call Dave and I 'the lads', which was a nice term of endearment. However, it got one young lady employee a bit confused of our friendship. She asked about how long we had known each other for, then saying that it's great that we met in college and to have found each other. HINT! Oh no, would be Dave's and my reaction, she was thinking we were a couple, so that rumour had to be quashed severely but it was highly unlikely that I, in the near future, would have a girlfriend to show.

A similar experience happened when Lee and I went to a pub together. As you are aware, it was difficult to stand for me and this pub was really busy. I truly wanted to leave as soon as I saw how crowded it was, but Lee saw a few seats free opposite to a married lady and gent. Lee asked if we could sit opposite and, seeing my condition, they did not hesitate. Lee came back moments later with drinks, and would then talk rather femininely. I was surprised as to this camp tone of voice coming from Lee's mouth, asking about breakfast in the morning. I immediately asked Lee to behave himself, as Lee had a great sense of humour and was adept at putting people on the spot. The couple opposite started to think that we were a couple as I saw panic in the gent's eyes. Lee continued, 'I think it would be nice to have cereal in the morning from Kellogg's, as it's lovely to see such a lovely cock in the morning!' My face went bright red, along with the couple opposite. Lee refrained from taking the joke any further but on reflection, it was funny yet also embarrassing for me. The married couple opposite rushed their drinks and the table became free; maybe that was Lee's intention?

I also hit a very important year; my 18th birthday. It was a huge celebration, which I saw a few years back for Ashley, and now it was my turn. It was celebrated in my home with so much food, and all the closest family were there to celebrate. It would be the icing on the cake for me when my organ teacher turned up, which surprised me totally, and then my Mum brought out a birthday cake in the shape of my organ. Note that I know you may be giggling on that last sentence. I had already heard so many organ puns of, "How big is your organ?" to the fact that it takes both hands to play with my organ! Anyway, back to the party, shall we! The ELECTRONIC organ cake was detailed in every way with the keys and buttons and pedals, and that which topped it off was that it was chocolate cake.

(My 18th Birthday Chocolate Organ Cake.)

Yummy! The present that I had from my parents was a huge red photo album; it looked like something which Eamonn Andrews brought in for 'This is Your Life'. The photos inside summed up my life perfectly; a baby with a huge head, childhood photos in plasters and in the swimming pool, or popular holidays we had together.

(Here I am on a family holiday wearing one of my favourite bands of all time, Meatloaf.)

This album stayed with me into adulthood to remember how things were, and to remind me how far along I have come with my family in those eighteen years.

It was in college and at music lessons that I began to develop a crush on a young lady who was a clarinettist. She was unusual to other ladies there; somewhat quirky with the choice of clothes, like cartoon figures on her t-shirts, and I liked that. During class, we would often talk and I was hoping that she was beginning to feel the same way. That's when I plucked up the courage and thought about how to ask her out. I did not want to ask her face-to-face. I did not think it was very courageous to ask a friend to ask on my behalf either. So, I found a possible telephone number in the directory and on a Saturday morning I, shakingly (I know it's a new word I've made up!), picked up the receiver, and dialled the number. She answered and it was definitely her voice, but she sounded somewhat confused as to what was going on. I mumbled nervously to ask just a few questions about music lessons and then I would summon up the question, "Do you want to meet up one evening?" It was then that I was sadly knocked for six when she advised she was not single. I thought she had kept that quiet in the time we had known each other. Once the telephone receiver was put down, I began to pull my hair out, literally, and mumble swear words as not to offend my Mum in the kitchen. That was the first, and last time I promised to myself, that I would ask a lady out on a date!

From the Monday onwards, being back at college was an embarrassment, I found it difficult to look into her eyes, and we had to work together still. In time, things grew back to normal and we remained just good friends.

Less than a year later, still at college, I heard from a friend of a friend that a young lady liked me. I did not know of her but, when I sat waiting in my car for a lesson, she made it obvious she was after me. It took a big indication for me to know that a lady was interested in me, like a tongue down my ear or something, otherwise I was oblivious. She stared into the car with interest as she walked slowly by with her friend, and that was another big indication. Well, I was embarrassed but thought she was attractive and had a Spanish look about her, which interested me. I agreed to try out a date, as a colleague asked on her behalf. It went well, so I thought, although in the bar she pointed out an ex-boyfriend in the crowd there, and it was somewhat uncomfortable. Yet we conversed well with each other and nervously touched an arm or a knee. Then we met another four times, and I started to hear from my sources that she was getting bored and that she wasn't too sure if I was really interested in her. It was time to go up another level and be less of a gentleman, I thought to myself. After one evening's drink together in a bar, I took a deviation away from her home. She was interested to know what I was up to. I was now eighteen and it was my first time of intimacy. We parked up in a church's car park late at night and the car windows got steamy, to say the least. Yet, in the back of my mind was the question of, "What am I doing?" There could be a mass murderer out there and attack us at the most vulnerable moment. The event was short-lived and I went to drop her off at home where she invited me in to go "all the way" but it had to be the right lady at the right time in my mind. It was all too much, and so I declined her invitation. From that moment, the relationship had ended in her eyes. I never got to know why she ignored me at college and did not return my calls. I felt somewhat that she was wanting one thing and that once that did not happen, it was no longer interesting to her, but I could not be too sure of that theory.

It was in this time that there was another lady I took an interest in. She worked at a local pub in Holbrook village, which sold lovely, flat, real ale as its speciality. It was a regular Sunday afternoon treat to have a pint or two and a natter with my Dad just before the huge Sunday lunch, plus trimmings, was devoured. However, the barmaid and I were beginning to chat and the conversation got more in-depth. I really wanted to take the matter further, but I was unsure if it was friendship or more and it was the biggest risk. It was to ask her out and lose both the friendship plus the venue for a pint with my Dad. So I never took the risk, and it was the one regret that, years later, reflecting on the matter, I thought that she may have really liked me. Plus, there was another chap (a good-looking guy) who also tried to gain her attention, and I felt that in no way would I win against this guy, so the chance slipped away.

Let's move away from a little thing called love, shall we? For the time being, anyway. In the college years, I found out about Motability (a car replacement scheme for disabled people) where I could have a new car every third year. I sold my little Astra and had a brand-new Ford Fiesta, which possibly made all the college students jealous. The funny thing about the assessment for me to get Disability Living Allowance at the age of eighteen, which allowed me to have mobility allowance, was that I, with my parents, went to a GP who did not know me as to make it a fair assessment. As I walked on crutches towards a long walk to the surgery, we got to a corner on a slope and a man nearly bumped into me as he was in such a rush. I nearly lost my balance and was held by my Dad to not go onto the road. The chap apologised and we continued on our way. I and my parents sat waiting for about ten minutes for the doctor to see me, when the door opened and it was the same chap that we had bumped into on the street moments before. He said that he could tell how difficult it was for me to move and he would not need to assess that side of walking, but continued to do other checks to fit the criteria.

Also, during the six week breaks during the college years, I had my first taste of work. My Dad managed to get me a job in a plastic factory where I would use machinery which made soap dispensers, toothbrushes, and so on. It was quick quality control work and paid well, which went towards paying back my old Astra car. The issues of me working there was the fact that my colleagues were mainly women, and therefore I was unable to connect with half of the conversations about soaps - the TV kind, not the soap dispensers at work, of course! Soap operas never existed in the Northridge household; just a few bars of the theme tune were enough to get the television turned over! It was deemed as dark and dismal in terms of the stories along with arguments constantly, and it served no purpose for the Northridges.

Anyway, back to the soap dispensers. The plastic was very hot and fast work; as soon as the items were in the hands the heat was disintegrating our cotton gloves provided. This brings me neatly on to the next point, which is that my hands are big and the sizes were supposed to fit all but, in my case, they were extremely tight. I can hear the thoughts going off in your head, big hands... Big organ, or big feet. Anyway, gloves were being replaced hourly to avoid burns from the hot plastic. It was not my ideal first job, but I thought it was impossible to do much else like delivering newspapers or washing cars.

Chapter 9

Northers Was Born

After another year at college, I gained four GCSEs and two A-Levels. My parents and I thought where to go next. It was a possible chance for University but, by then, I had had enough of studying, plus the qualifications needed to incorporate a Maths GCSE. That idea went out as quickly as it came in. So it was the next thing; what work did I want to do? There was no question about it. It simply had to involve music. During that short period of time of looking in the papers, applying for certain jobs, getting some interviews, even one as a music therapist for a special needs school. Sometimes I had no interviews at all, so I decided to lower expectations and to have a job, any job, to bring in some money. My Dad got involved, again, to help, and this time it was a chocolate factory which my Dad had sold oil to. It was near to where I lived and it paid well. Even with my Dad's connections, I had to have an interview and trial to see how I would perform. It went well and I was asked to join the company the very next day.

The place was huge, with many factory belts running off with different types of chocolate boxes. The smell of chocolate hit me like an aroma of love. It was a place that was perfect for the time being. It was not an easy place, as the packing of chocolate was a fast moving line, but I was very good at playing the organ meaning I had a quick hand and eye coordination. The best part of working there was the fact that you could actually sample what was being packed and, in fact, the managers insisted that someone should try them to see if any faulty produce was made. So I sampled, sampled, and sampled some more. It was an even better day when it was time to pack liquor chocolates so I could get slightly drunk at the same time. It was a bad day if the chocolates were diabetic and to try them would mean many trips to the toilet, so refraining from that unusual chocolate was the key. But, at break times, I would visit a colleague, look interested whilst talking, and eat their chocolate instead!

There were negatives to the job, and they were that it was extremely repetitive, and it also depended on who sat next to me. It was a bad day if I had to sit with someone that irritated me by being talked at me, and not to me. Plus, the local radio station was only allowed to be on for four hours in total throughout the day. There were some people there that behaved like children, for example, there would be regular occurrence where someone shouted down the belt for all to hear, "Not long now!" to which they would have the response back from many folks of, "It's Christmas!" They were trying their best to do to the nearest impersonation of Noddy Holder. Now it would be ok, but this was in September or, on extreme occasions, it was in January as the Christmas chocolates went to the deep freeze section.

I thought to myself that there were also some highly-intelligent folks there who had lost their previous jobs and doing this work for a few weeks helped somewhat. Sometimes I could have a chat with one person who had degrees and yet he or she was sitting next to me or the Christmas-obsessed factory lot. I also sat next to one guy called Mo who originated from Egypt; the stories he told about how it was better to be living in the UK made time fly whilst packing the little chocolates. The day became a terrible day if you discovered you were off to work in the toffee room. The reason being was that ear defenders had to be worn to protect your ears from the noise of breaking toffee. The boxes of toffee advertised that it was broken by hand and, indeed it was, but with small toffee hammers. This did not go down well for my large hands as it became tiring to hold and bash away. It also made it worse if the person you were chopping for was packing too much in each box, therefore being unable to keep up. I was shouting across, "Oi, slow down!" However, the banging of the toffee hammers made it difficult to get the point across. The best technique was to get the slab of toffee and then slam (unless it was fruit and nut which was impossible to break up unless Semtex was used!) it on to the table to cause as much damage as possible. After this, unwrap the toffee and bash away like crazy. With the ear defenders on, no-one could have a decent conversation, and neither could they hear the radio. The next thing to happen which made the day go from bad to worse was that the toffee ripped into the plastic gloves, cutting the hands, which stopped everything on the belt (and that happened all too regularly) to have blue plasters put on. To add insult to injury, it was pretty bad for the guys or, in some cases the girls, if they had a hairy chest, as fragments of toffee would penetrate the factory aprons and onto skin and hair. I had wonderful times of pulling out the toffee after work and had something to nibble on after dinner. Another negative was the six minute toilet break, giving me no chance to dash over, so I kept it all in until the thirty minute lunch or thirteen minute breakfast/afternoon breaks. Sometimes I ate too much chocolate so then I would not need the lunch break to eat. Also, my uncle Roy worked as an electrician there until he retired so occasionally we'd get to have a chat in the canteen. The whole time-keeping was done via clocking in and out which was typical of factory work. Also, it was funny to see people outside of work without their uniforms. It was funny to see how people looked without the hairnet and hat, either with or without hair.

There were other jobs which were also difficult for me, like making the chocolate boxes, which required nimble hands. Then there was sending the plastic trays down the line for people to pack into, and these were called formers. There were inspecting jobs too but, in my time there, I was never unleashed to do that. Then lidding (another new word in the dictionary!) the boxes to sealing them, putting stickers and bows on them. It was an amazing amount of folks to make a single box of chocolate and I did not see the process of how chocolates were made either, but I left that to the Oompa Loompas!

For a job which I thought would be temporary, it became permanent. In fact, it was my job for four years and I put on so much weight; two stone, to be precise. It was a job that was not too stressful but had a fast tempo, where I still had energy to do things in the evening. I made new friends on the way also, like Marky and John, where all will become clear a little bit later.

So, after I came home from work, I was practising on the organ and, with the money I made in the factory, I bought keyboards and speakers. One evening, an advert in the local newspaper caught my eye. It was an advert asking for a keyboard player for a Rock band called Jinx. Perfect, I thought, and set up an audition. This went well, as I performed parts from my Grade 8 like 'The Arrival of the Queen of Sheba', which was a fast-finger tune that looks impressive. Their band consisted of Chris on bass guitar, Chris on the drums (but he was sadly replaced as sometimes tempo was lost, making it hard for the band, so later Steve joined as the drummer), John on guitar who did both rhythm and lead, and then two singers - Serena and Diane. Their music was mainly covers of bands such as Fleetwood Mac and Rock-y types like Bryan Adam's 'Summer of 69'. They thought that I would suit the band, and we rehearsed together. Before I knew it, I was gigging with the band and thoroughly enjoyed the music. We did concerts both locally and as far as London. The band made a demo in a professional recording studio and I created a stage name of Paul Cadenza. Cadenza was derived from an Italian music term, which was a showing-off bit for a soloist. It was a name which was a bit extreme for my character, but the sound of it was much better than Northridge. It gave me a feeling that I was Italian, especially with facially-looking a bit similar with dark hair.

Jinx had cat eyes as a logo on all their artwork, and that looked very eye-catching. The band had a look of that like Fleetwood Mac, specifically with Diane both sounding and looking like Stevie Nicks. We did other songs such as 'Circle in the Sand' by Belinda Carlisle and 'Hold the Line' by Toto, which brings me neatly to the Battle of the Bands night.

The band entered the competition, which was for local bands to battle it out in front of judges. Jinx's night was against four other bands. We were favouring ourselves as winners when we listened to most of the competition, especially one which had a guitarist that unfortunately snapped a string, meaning that they had to restart the song after repairing it. When it was Jinx's turn to go, there was an issue of my right hand freezing for two reasons; one, the toffee hammer which had been used for four hours in the factory prior to the concert had made my wrist stiffen and two, I began to feel stage fright. I had never experienced that ever before; not once experienced on the stage of the Miners Welfare, not once of all the gigs at caravan clubs, nor at my Grade 8 exam. My 'Hold the Line' piano solo with fast chords in triplets went pear-shaped completely. This ended Jinx's chance of winning. Nothing was said about the incident, but I knew the finger pointed straight at me. Anyway, I continued to perform gigs with the band and 'Hold the Line' was sometimes omitted from the gig list. It was a sad moment, though, that when John the guitarist stated he had to leave due to family commitments, and that marked the beginning of the end for Jinx. We tried with other guitarists, but no-one could be as good as John, and then we all disbanded after two years of me being with the band. The two young ladies created an Abba cover band and made more of a successful career of it. Steve the drummer fruitfully joined another local band, and I also kept in contact with him.

So, back to my day job, the chocolate factory which was nothing like Dahl's Wonka's by the way, unless the Oompa Loompas made the chocolates. A chap sat next to me who I had never seen before, or so we thought, and he introduced himself to me as Mark. We began to talk and, in a short period of time, found out a common link of the love of music. From there we found out that we both played instruments, that we were both in bands, and then I found out that he too was in the Battle of the Bands. In fact, he was the unlucky guitarist who had snapped his string. From then on, we formed a strong bond. We shared many hours on the belts together. The days would whizz by, talking about music and more. When we had nothing to say, then competitions were designed such as guessing the song to a lyric or naming the song by asking questions about the singer, and so on. Eventually, nicknames were introduced, and Mark was either 'Marky' or 'Lil', and I was 'Northers' which another pal, Dave (old college buddy), was already calling me. 'Northers' derived from a cricket term, since Dave loved the sport. So, Dave shortened Northridge and I found it unusual but I liked it, so 'Northers' was born.

Another pal came into view called John. Lovely chap, one of the quiet guys who preferred to listen than speak, but when he spoke, all would listen to him. John was in a relationship, so very few people got to know him outside of work. John had his own nickname for me and that was 'Sex Machine'. In John's eyes, I was attracting members of the opposite sex. In my own eyes I wasn't too sure of that fact as I was still single. I was not a bad-looking chap, according to a few ladies who stated such, although I was not keen on those trying their hardest to catch my attention, as desperation was not interesting to me. One lady did catch my attention who was a new starter. I plucked up the courage to make conversation whilst packing chocolates together and we seemed to hit it off. We connected so much so that we flirted all the time with each other. However, in conversation, it was realised that she was in a relationship, so I still flirted but would not dare to ask her out, especially how my first attempt at college was a huge flop. The flirting happened outside of work also, as I saw her walking to work one morning and it began to be a regular occurrence where I would pick her up in my car at that specific junction before making our way to work together to the factory. That was until one day where my pal, Marky, who also had a crush on this lady, went one stage further by picking her up from her home so that was the end of that. Not long afterwards, the news was announced that she and Mark were a couple. I was shocked and thought I should have moved faster. It could be possibly seen that Mark and I should have ended our friendship over this lady, but I was really seeing beyond that, plus I valued his friendship. However, I had another lady - who shall remain nameless - who flirted with me who, again, had a boyfriend and, again, I would not make the move as to cause embarrassment to myself. It was fun to make it difficult for her to pack chocolates by moving her chocolates away, just so that she would end up against my body in desperation to catch up. This was liked by us both as it was seen by others at work and arose to colleagues that we could have been a couple. Sadly, it was the fact that I was not sure of asking someone out and lacked in the 'asking out' department that we weren't a couple, only due to the first and last time of asking a girl out as per my college experience.

There was another moment that affected me with my thoughts about relationships, causing me to be extremely cautious. A collection of friends and I from work decided to go out for a Friday night drink together. I drove and did not mind being sober, driving my friends into and out of town, back to their homes. The night went well. Our group of colleagues were a bit to very drunk that night. It was time for me now to taxi them back home, and four people in total were cramped into the car. It turned out a bad choice for me that I took a route back which meant one lady was the last to be dropped off.

Now, I will be totally honest, I did not know this young lady very well but, whilst driving, we made small talk, although the conversation went deeper. She stated about her boyfriend who she wanted to break up from. I was trying to help as much as possible, although had very little wisdom to draw upon in relationships. I eventually ended up outside the lady's home and she was still pouring her heart out in a drunken stupor. I was itching to get back home as it was getting late, plus I had work the next day (it was my second job as a music teacher, which will be mentioned later), so I was trying politely to end the chat. The next moment was that the boyfriend of the lady was outside the car, and he proceeded to drag her out. She ended up on the pavement and he made his way into my car to beat me up. He first headbutted me and then flung punches at me in the cramped car space. It was a fight or flight moment. I decided to fly. I held back this drunken, enraged boyfriend with my strong left arm and started the car with my right hand. The car began to set off with the guy still in the passenger side until he could not keep up, as his legs were outside, so he fell out eventually. However, the car's open passenger door hit two parked cars in the kerfuffle. With my adrenaline pumping throughout my body, how I got home and how I managed to get the car into the garage was a mystery later. I closed the garage door, suspiciously looking around, as maybe this maniac had followed me. I went into my home to my parent's bedroom whilst they slept and then woke them. I told them of the crazy situation. My parents saw the bruises around my neck from where the man had grabbed it, my bruised fat lips, and a black eye puffing up like Mike Tyson had had a go at me.

My parents tried their best to make sure the madman had not followed me, and they calmed me with a stiff drink. I managed to sleep somewhat that night, under my parent's protection, but the next day was more of a nightmare with the car that I loved being damaged so much. My Dad reported the incident to the police who replied, "Funny that, because there were two cars damaged that night". It was explained that I hit them by accident that night. I had to make a statement in the police station, and so off my Dad and I drove in my beaten-up car. The bumper dragged along the road and this, along with my broken face, was a sight to behold to onlookers, as we could not drive very fast.

The sergeant asked for a statement, and I said it how it was. I was then asked if I wanted to press any charges. I discussed the matter and thought it would be complicated seeing the young lady at work, as she would hold me responsible of charging her boyfriend or potentially ex-boyfriend, at least. So, it was deemed better not to press charges. It was with this bruised face and damaged emotions that I thought I could not go to teach, however, after an encouraging conversation with my Dad, I decided not to cancel the lessons. It was not surprising that the pupils were more interested in studying my face rather than the notes on the music book. The time went by and I focused on the lessons and put the problems behind me, so it was a wise choice by my Dad.

The Monday swiftly arrived and I had to go back at the factory. In the men's changing room, the larger chaps who worked in the warehouse side of things were shocked and wanted to know what had happened and who did it. Basically, the chaps in the warehouse wanted blood. Granddad Ron had wanted blood too, but my parents and I thought it was not the way to go. I went onto the belt, where the young lady who was involved in the event was so shocked to see my face that she became hysterical. She wanted to make sure that he, the boyfriend, would pay for the car excess of insurance and, indeed, the payments came through, but I suspected it was she who paid me back.

The lesson to be learnt here was to be really careful of

who to take in my car and that jealousy is a dangerous thing, even when not being naughty and it was just a mistake. To be frank, I would have understood more if she and I were doing something incorrect, but it was all a big mistake. It would make me feel even more slower to approach the opposite sex, especially if they were with a partner. However, the experience did make me cautious, but I still wanted to try to gain a lady in my life.

I joined dating agencies and advertised myself in the single columns in the local newspapers. It was remarkable that I would play around a bit with my style. I was, at first, completely honest and said that I was disabled, but only two replies came from that. Then, the same advert went out again a month later without stating about a disability and I had about ten replies. That kind of gave me the sense that ladies did not want the baggage of a chap who is disabled. Now, there was one lady who replied to the original advert, so I thought to give it a go. The conversation over the telephone was a nervous one, of course, and the lady said she was on the large side, but it did not concern me. We arranged to meet in a car park of a pub and go from there. I got to the car park ten minutes early as I had a thing about being in good time and hated to be late. I waited, waited, and waited some more and before I knew it, she was either twenty minutes late or was never going to show up. I turned on the ignition and, at that very moment, a lady started to walk towards my car. She was rather larger than I thought she was going to be, wearing a denim mini skirt and a lycra top which had a very low plunging neckline. Needless to say, the way she presented herself did not match to my tastes, but we were here now, and I thought to give her the benefit of the doubt. The conversation was extremely difficult, as she mentioned all the soap operas that she liked to watch on TV, which I detested so much. She then boasted about how many burgers she could eat in one day, which was not impressing me in the slightest. However, the conversation killer of the night was that her hobbies included throwing frisbees. I enquired whether she had a dog to play such with, but "No," she replied, "I just like to throw frisbees". With conversation already being out of the question, I knew that we were not meant to be. I decided to take her to a pub and play pool, so that at least then we were not sitting and talking. That was a bad idea, as the plunging neckline on her top was not what I wanted to see, and it brought a lot of attention to the public, so the next idea was to take her to the cinema. It was a chick-flick called 'Mirror Has Two Faces' and it was as dull as the date in my mind. However, the lady (from the date) drank the large cola within thirty minutes of the film starting. I could hear the empty straw still trying to reach the remaining bits of cola which was getting people's heads turning. I just had to buy her another drink otherwise it would be uproar in the cinema. I told her to keep watching the film and I would buy another cola. The queue for drinks was quite long and by the time I got to order a drink, she came running out, thinking that I had left her there. The film eventually finished, and then it was a long journey back with the lady asking questions of planning the next date which I felt awkward to be brutally honest and say it won't happen, so I went along with her plans. She asked for a kiss when we pulled up near to her home and I could not disappoint, so when she got nearer I turned so she kissed my cheek. When she called on the phone a day or so later, my parents answered with planned tactics saying that I had gone to work in Spain and that they were not sure when I would be back.

I had a few more dates, mainly set up by dating agencies, and the ladies were mainly shocked about how severe my disability was. It was my gut instinct, as I was good at judging reactions. It was a standard answer that I got as to be dumped which was, "You're too nice" or "You're too tactile ". I heard it once too many times and thought to myself or whether they wanted a man who would swear and hit them about a bit. It was just a ploy to avoid the disabled bit and to not break my heart, but it was transparent.

This is when a thought occurred to me to date disabled ladies, perhaps. However, when I saw a small amount of the Paralympics on the TV, it was like looking in a mirror. It made me feel sick to my stomach. The thought of seeing another disabled body just repulsed me, and that was the end of that thought.

From my early years, I felt that I was walking normally and that there wasn't any limping involved, only to catch a glimpse of myself in action, which knocked my viewpoint of myself completely. I also tried to disguise the way I walked and my body shape by having my shirt not tucked into my trousers, so that the shirt covered over my bottom.

One thing that made me feel normal, which I looked for more often than not, was to be liked by the opposite sex. For example, I could be driving in my car and there would be an attractive lady in her car, and if she smiled at me to suggest she thought I was cute then it gave me great feelings. Even at a stag do with Mark (yes, Mark and this lady tied the knot) and other friends, I was the only one that "pulled" as, while I sat talking in a pub in Blackpool, a lady made a beeline to me. We hit it off and had a few kisses and cuddles. However, when I got up to move onto another pub, that was the end of that; perhaps it was ugly to her to see me standing or some other reason, who knows. Yet the stag do group kept calling me "Northers, the man!"

That's another thing; why do a pub crawl? I was quite happy sitting in one place as there was music, beer, people coming and going, and it was never dull. Yet Mark's friends thought the grass was greener elsewhere, so off they'd go to about five pubs in one night. This complicated things; finding seats, trying to go through a crowded pub, and treading on those people's toes who did not move fast enough. Later at night, I'd be trying to avoid the sick on the floor as the crutches and wet fluids would equal another fall and a bruised arse! People got so drunk that they just bumped into me as I was trying my best to get out of a crowded place with the pounding bass music which continued to pound in my head as I drove back home.

A thought would often occur when seeing the same old faces every week who were obviously single, getting pie-eyed, and trying to hit on some younger person. Was that going to happen to me? Occasionally I would "pull" and not always for the better; sometimes it was a much older lady who would not understand, due to alcohol numbness, that I was not interested, plus I was too polite to say "go away!" There had also been men showing interest in me which would often amuse my pals with their remarks of, "Northers, you were in there mate," or "you should have gone for it!" I did not want to be judgemental in sexual preferences - each to their own - but when it was being pushed onto me, then I would have to show strongly that I was not interested by staring at nearby ladies.

Chapter 10

Zuckermans famous Pig

Back to the factory. In the four years of working in the factory, other events in my family life occurred. One was when I went on holiday to visit my pal, Lee, in Mablethorpe. The holiday was my first long distance drive, which was interesting to see where my driving skills would take me. It was a great time, catching up with Lee, staying in a caravan by myself, and watching the shows in the evening where Lee performed. It was my first holiday without my parents being around, so an aspect of freedom was felt. I kept in touch with my parents and made sure to check in with, "I'm ok" as they worried for this first away trip. However, in the conversations in that week with my parents, I felt something was not quite right. Now, I am not a fortune teller of any kind; every now and then I have a little intuition, but that was all. For example, as a four year old boy, I was shopping with my mum and, in a corridor between two shops, I had a glimpse that something terrible was going to happen and I had to run out from this corridor. The reason will become clear in this book later. On my return back from my Mablethorpe holiday which I felt I had to cut short a little, I was given the sad news which I was dreading to hear; my Mum had breast cancer.

At this moment, it was a depression that I could not avoid. She was the figure in my life that had steered me to being the character I had become. She was the lady in my life that I could always talk to for any guidance, reassurance, to have a cuddle when I needed it, to have the feeling of real love and compassion, and now that was threatened to be taken away from me. Now, I had to pull on my resources, act brave, and not to let my concerns be known. I had already seen my Granddad pass away from cancer, and it was now possibly the same for my Mum.

Mum also hit rock bottom at one point with her own concerns and the 'what ifs'. I took her outside to sit on the patio bench in the sunshine. Words flowed out from my heart; words that could not be remembered if you asked what had been said. It was just from my heart to my Mum's and she absorbed my feelings of positivity, feelings of hope, and feelings of perseverance. It was just like the heart-to-hearts that Mum had given to me on my low days when I was tired of trying more at physiotherapy or when I was tired of the other children who did not allow me to be involved.

This conversation on the patio fed Mum's spirit and gave her the courage to fight on. She was later to have the cancerous lump removed and began radiotherapy. During Mum's time in hospital, Dad broke down and it was me who gave him a man's hug. I had never seen my Dad in tears before, well, apart from when he watched 'This is Your Life' on the television where, every week, he had to have a box of tissues standing by! I also gave my Dad words of hope and reassurance hugs. Together, as family, we are fighting this cancer, was the thought pulsating through my heart. It was a difficult time for all to know if the treatment was working and whether they had caught it in the early stages. The treatment Mum had been given was a tiring one and very sore for her skin but, with the support of her family behind her, it would be her way to a strong recovery. Surely enough, she bounced back to full health. My Mum had regular check-ups and eventually she was given the all-clear. I must say it hit me into pure reality of the possibility of losing my Mum and, secretively, I was still at rock bottom during that period of recovery.

I was encouraged when I heard that a few of my colleagues at the chocolate factory were arranging an evening out to see Wayne Anthony, a local clairvoyant. I had never been to one before and was sceptical, but I needed some hope in my life. Wayne met me and, in the first few moments, was accurately stating that my Mum was ill, that it was cancer, and it was of the breast. I was in shock by those lines and it washed away any negative views I had. Wayne continued to state that my Mum was going to be ok and probably said too much when he commented that she was going to live longer than my Dad, which was something I did not want to know about. He went on to say more about how many times I would move homes and how many times I would marry and that I would be strongly connected to Russia. By that point, I thought Wayne was losing the plot. By seeing Wayne, it encouraged me to see another clairvoyant, and this time it was a lady. I was curious as to what would be said differently. She mentioned about marrying five times, moving house about eight times, and that my condition will improve by medicine. On that visit, I was more negative as to what clairvoyants knew, yet Wayne was spot on.

After meeting with Wayne Anthony and with him knowing all that information, I saw him as an amazing guy and I told so many people at work about my experiences with a level of accuracy. I also felt that my Mum would be safe and well. However, I was confused with the fact of ever seeing myself to be married, and thought it impossible. I'll be honest, looking back at my near-death experience, I remember seeing views of Russia, like the Kremlin but, again, it was a 14-year-old boy confused as hell with what he saw. Plus, there were no moments of a white wedding seen in the NDE.

Going back to the time when my Mum had cancer, I also had a problem with my back ever since the journey to and from Mablethorpe, as long periods in a car stiffened my back. I decided to go to a lady who helped my Mum in the past with a slipped disc. She massaged my unusual back, but it was not helping in any way. So, out came the needles! It was for acupuncture, which she also practiced in. Now, I had needles galore in my life, and it was not a pain for me to have more, so I told the lady to give it a go. The pain of the thinnest needles going in was not at all so bad, kind of like a bee sting, and then the needles stay for a length of time. During this, I mentioned about my low feelings in emotion and Mum's cancer, and that's when she mentioned that acupuncture can help for that also. She asked if it was ok to have one more needle in, near to my wrist, to which I agreed. Now the back took a bit of time to adjust and get right, eventually, but I was beginning to feel like a new man emotionally. The needle near to the hand was amazing, but it gave me the feelings of being somewhat drunk. The question was; was the needle coated in anything? It was not, of course! I had to sit in my car outside for a bit of time before I could drive, as the feelings lasted for quite some time. It was then that I could give words of hope and encouragement to fight this and, to my friends at work, they strongly suspected that I had something like an addiction. Why was I so jolly when they knew of my Mum's cancer?! Life became normal again and the scare had died down, but it gave a huge shock and wake-up to all of the family of how delicate life can be.

I still worked in the chocolate factory when Jinx (my first band) disbanded, and it was discussed between us that Marky and I were to join forces to make music. Mark was a great singer and songwriter. He had his unique type of writing which could not really be likened to any other. Marky and I rehearsed in my bedroom weekly and, when we were ready to perform, we mainly performed at open mic sessions at folk clubs. That got us onto performing as warm-up artists for main acts. Our duo was called 'Zuckerman's Famous Pig', yes, it was a name which is easy to forget and we were always to be asked twice what the band was called by people asking about it. The title came from the book/film 'Charlotte's Web', which Marky liked so much. Marky and I later started to perform our own concerts and the audience consisted of friends, family, colleagues, and new faces. We later appeared on a local radio station and performed live which was nerve-wracking for us both, but we did it and we were proud. Later, we enrolled a penny whistle chap who gave solos in the music, giving Marky a break from singing all the time. The band got disbanded a little bit later naturally, but Marky and I remained as close pals.

Chapter 11

Playing With My Organ

Packing chocolates helped in many ways; I met new friends, connected with the fairer sex, it helped with money, was not too much of a stressful job, and enabled me to work in different bands. However, it had to come to an end as I was thinking I could do so much more with my life, and it was a mind-numbing job, to be honest. I applied for a job as a music teacher for a music shop in the centre of Derby; see that I mentioned it before, when I was beaten up on that Friday night? I had an interview at this music shop and then a second interview where I had to perform music. It was 'Tico Tico' and my favourite, 'The Arrival of the Queen of Sheba'. I got the job and, from building up my lessons there, I managed to hand my notice in at the factory.

Teaching was great fun for me and I could connect with so many people. Have a laugh and a joke, learn about what made my pupils tick, and to try to inspire them to play an instrument. So many pupils came and went as was the usual events for a teacher. The issues of a child not wanting to practice happened so much. Or it could be the parents who are struggling to pay, but embarrassed to say about it. Or it could be those children who thought it would be just a few lessons to play like Liberace but the realisation of hard work was too much. Or it could be the pushy parents who wished they had the chance when they were younger, so they lived their love of music through their child, although it was not loved by their child.

I designed my studio into something that would interest the children with colourful and textured photo frames that had new photos in every week. I would design music sheets with quizzes and jokes for the children to take away to enjoy. I would have my regular pupils who I connected with so well and give them unconditional support so that they could be themselves, and did not have to hide away that they could not practice for whatever reason. They knew they would not be chastised, but I had to tell off a few children who thought they could do what they wanted. Some children used my kind nature, but they learnt that it was not possible when I gave them 'the look', which would make them think that I am not always that kind guy. I also found out about each child as to what they wanted to play, and I would then come back a few weeks later with that music. This music was adapted by me so it would be easy for the child to pick up and learn, giving them something fun to play and not just 'Ode to Joy'.

Then, it would be the adults in the daytime that I would teach during the week. It would be the pensioners who wanted to learn but did not have the money when they were children themselves. Then it was the younger adults who also missed it as children and wished they'd carried on. Again, I was inspiring to both the young and old wanting so much to reach their goal. In the building where I taught there were about another four teachers and studios. I had the top floor studio; yes, a guy with poorly legs was on the top floor. It was difficult for the manager to move the teachers who had worked at the place for many years prior to me joining so I 'reached the top and stayed there' until it was time to go home.

I was still embarrassed by my legs and, with having children in my studio, I was not brilliant to disguise my disability, so an office chair which I could wheel backwards and forwards was a great help. Maybe the children had ideas that I could not walk well, especially with how my shoes were different to anyone else's, but I was not there to show my walking difficulties to them and that was how it stayed. Another difficulty that raised its ugly head was the issue of teaching rhythm. My first teacher, from the age of 11 to 14, really did help me to read music and to practice fingering. I would listen to my teacher perform the next piece of music which inspired me to practice, but it was neglecting how to learn rhythm. I must give you a fact that I had sailed pass all seven books in the series with my first teacher. When it came to change to another teacher, Tim Flint, and he heard me play for the first time, he immediately asked me where my rhythm was. I said that I was not taught it. Immediately, I went back to book one. So, rhythm was not natural for me, and to explain it to students was extremely difficult. The other part was musical expression; I had not learnt expression so much as I was not able to use the swell pedal on the organ which controlled the volume, thus giving me very little content in my own lessons. Lessons were pleasurable for both teacher and pupil, but I knew that I had my own limitations and that it would not be my full career in the end. By the way, it was not for the fact that my parents didn't try to help me play with expression. They invited people to design an adaptation which fixed on to the swell pedal and to come up via a swivel for my right knee but, because my hip was limited in movement, my whole body had to move to create the dynamics, which was uncomfortable to play. There was then another idea to put a similar device under my bottom cheek and it was, again, difficult to move and play so I played without the dynamics in the end. In later years, I thought it was the wrong instrument to pick up and that maybe piano would have suited more, but there were pedals there too. Hindsight is not a good thing to look back on, or I could have learned saxophone!

In this period of time of being a teacher, I had the freedom to come and go. I could cancel lessons when something else had to happen instead, so there was a lot of flexibility which was a bonus that I loved. I was also teaching privately, and one gentleman was a terrific chap. He was in his early eighties when I started to teach him, although he had had lessons before from another local teacher. I did not ask for much in the sense of finance as I just enjoyed his company, his love of music, and his wife's cakes when they were brought to me during the lessons. I think I taught this gentleman for about two years, and he would always walk with me to the car to wave goodbye. The strangest thing was that I had a feeling which came to me saying that was the last time I was going to see him. It was correct, as I had a call a few days later from his very upset wife. Maybe it's because of my Near-Death Experience that I have been given some gifts or that I just naturally sense some things, it's hard to say really. There is one other strange thing that I would like to bring to your attention which has happened twice in my life. I was driving, once in the London area when I saw my brother and the second instance was near to where I lived. What I am talking about was that I was at junctions, looked both ways a few times to ensure it was clear then suddenly, as I am moving out, a car quickly approaches me. The next thing is that I just felt lifted and moved across slightly as to avoid the on-coming vehicle. This is strange, even for me to write this down, and I am probably going to lose a few readers now as they'll think I am nuts. If I don't write it either, then I feel like I am not being totally open with you. Now, to explain the car incidents in my mind, it feels like something was trying to wipe me out but then something else decided, no it's not my time to go, and stopped this 'bad energy/elements' from succeeding. I'll go one stage further and say that, since my Near-Death Experience at the age of 14, I was thinking that the universe is all energy. We are energy, and there is a consciousness that we all share. We live in a holographic universe. Now, it's not just me that had said this, as even mainstream science has stated it too. Everything is atoms; Einstein said that and, for what it is worth, I agree with that. Things are atoms but based on a low energy, so a table/chair is solid to how we feel it but basically, it's all atoms still but condensed. I hope it helps readers to go out there and investigate for yourselves as it's important, and that's why I need to say these things.

In this time of my life, when I was a music teacher, my Granddad Ron passed away. Sadly, Ron died too young like all great people as he was plagued by heart attacks; some of which he would not tell a soul about, even his wife until later on. His triple bypass operation that he had seemed to do the trick but, during the weeks on the way to recovery, he passed away at his home. Ron was a warm, quiet guy with very high intelligence and he would love to spend time doing crosswords or making his model steam engines with a village.

(Granddad Ron and I having a laugh together during a family barbeque.)

On the day of his funeral, it was wintery but with a blue sky. Ashley helped to carry Ron, being a pall-bearer, and it was a lovely ceremony as the priest knew Ron very well. During the funeral, Ashley did a lovely speech about Ron. Ashley remarked on his humour and the enjoyment of getting people drunk. Throughout the time in the church, I noticed a chap looking at me and it reminded me of a Primary School teacher who I did not connect with at all.

It was that teacher who did not know how to look after a child with a disability. I was certain that it was him, but time flew and people changed. I thought that the teacher would not recognise me for sure as I was not that ten year old boy anymore, but how I walked gave it all away. The teacher made a beeline to shake Ashley's hand and then mine once the ceremony had finished. I was embarrassed to shake his hand, no, it was more of a resentment to shake his hand, but I did not want to make a scene on this sad occasion, nor did I want to hold a grudge.

The ceremony in the church had finished, and the congregation made their way to the place of burial which was on a steep hill with wet grass and a lot of folks, including me, stayed nearby but on the path. I wished so very much that I could get up close to say my final words to Ron but I knew that it would mean me falling over for sure. The coffin bearers themselves staggered to reach that point and it made the entire congregation very concerned. I could not hear the priest at all, as the wind threw the words up into the sky. I took a moment to think of the great times with Ron. The time when Ron saw a mouse on the patio and he took a pebble to toss into the air just to make it run away but the pebble landed right on the mouse's head, killing it instantly. He was gutted and he had to bury it, all the time apologising to the poor little mouse. It was on my mind when Ron chased me around the garden and we were in fits of laughter. At that moment of reflection, a robin redbreast stood right next to me just a metre away and I wondered whether it was Ron in another form. It was crazy, but we both could not stop looking at each other. Sadly, the robin went when the coffin was lowered into the ground. In my thoughts, I gave Ron a sad farewell but a big thank you for everything he did for me and for being a wonderful Granddad. I would reflect upon Ron at the times I drove past the graveyard and send him the warmest "hello". I had a pocket watch which Ron gave me a year before he passed away and his World War II badge that he gave me a few years before also which I reflected upon.

After the funeral, everyone made their way to the pub for the wake. People shared their memories of Ron and family caught up on lost time, as it was ages for some to see each other. I kept seeing the teacher who was mentioned at the church. I kept busy and avoided a conversation with the teacher. Once the food and drinks had ended, people made their way home. My family and I went back to my Nana's home as we did not want to leave Nana so soon. We were all drinking tea and coffee, reflecting on a beautiful ceremony that Ron would have been proud of, when the phone rang. Ashley answered it on Nana's behalf, spoke for a good few minutes, and then announced to me that the phone call was for me to take. I whispered to my brother as to enquire who was on the other end of the phone and it was that very same teacher. I struggled to put the phone to my ear and say hello, however I could not ignore it. The voice on the other end was warm and the conversation mainly consisted of the teacher talking to me as I was lost for words of kindness for my old teacher. The teacher wanted to say that he saw that I had grown up into a wonderful young man and it was a pleasure to see me. I knew that this was the nearest thing to an apology and I absorbed the words which gave me warmth. These words buried any ill feelings that I had at that time.

Back to the subject of work; being a teacher gave me flexible time to do other things in my life. For example, I continued to play the organ/keyboard in many different places like in Miner Welfares, Social Clubs, Caravan Clubs, stroke clubs, and nursing homes. Let me give you a few small stories about these times in my life. Now, I could not remember music very well at all, and I was envious of people who could just turn up with their instrument and play, like my pal Lee. Lee could play piano for hours without a single book in front of him and just merge one song into another. What I would do was bring at least two large briefcases with music wherever I went. As the applause would happen after I finished one piece of music, I would then get the next one ready. I had a unique style of playing though; I would play a piece of music differently each time I played it. I loved to improvise and, thinking about it, it was not dull to the listeners as I would change it somewhat, nor dull for myself too. Improvising skills were taught to me by Tim Flint, as this also did not come naturally.

One time, when I used to play for the elderly people in nursing homes, I would don my suit, and get out the singalong tunes like 'Lambeth Walk' and 'Hokey Cokey', which would rarely get anyone singing or dancing as most of the people were asleep. However, on one occasion, one very nice lady sat right next to me and smiled. She asked me about what I was going to do and play, so I told her politely that I was going to play some sing-a-long tunes. The lady replied with positivity and stated that she could not wait to hear me. As soon as I was set up and ready to play my first piece, she applauded excitedly. I played a Frank Sinatra piece of 'New York, New York' and she said to me that I was very good, that she loved it, but told me that I could now go home. She had heard enough. I did not know what to do as I had been invited to play for two hours. I ignored her wish to leave and played another piece of 'Carolina Moon'. She said afterwards with a dark, menacing tone, "I said you are very good, but you can go home now, thank YOU!" I was unnerved with the lady next to me. I asked the carers if I could have a break, as they said that maybe she'll get bored and go to her room. Surely enough, after twenty minutes' tea break, she did and I finished the set off.

Now, the next bit is not for the faint-hearted. I came home and wanted to change from my suit into casual wear. I took off my jacket and hung it on the coat hanger. Then, off came the trousers. I was by myself at home and often did the same thing; I put the coat hanger hook between my teeth whilst threading the trousers through. On this occasion, though, the hook removed itself from the teeth and settled right behind into the fleshy area underneath my gum. With the coat hanger glued to my mouth, I gave an almighty yelp of pain that the whole village must have heard as I proceeded to gently pull it out, thus leaving a hole in my mouth, and it was so sore. I went to the local hospital where they advised I would need to gargle regularly with a solution until it eventually healed up. The message is: Do not hold coat hangers by your teeth.

Chapter 12

Thank You Sue

So, one day, whilst still being a teacher and giving my all for the pupils, for whatever reason, I had hit rock bottom. I was seeing myself as not a human being, as incapable of being loved unless by a friend or family member, and not an object of desire to the opposite sex. To be someone who is entertaining to children as a clown when I was walking or standing. To know that I will never be able to do the things I wanted to do, never be able to be the man I dreamed of being. The depression swam around my whole body and mind, and it engulfed me completely. It would not be seen by others, it must not be seen by others, as I demanded of myself not to look weak. I even hid it well from my parents. It was the straw that broke the camel's back when a lad just asked the question, "what happened with you?" and the young boy got chastised by his embarrassed mum for asking such a question in the supermarket. This question had been asked a million times (or at least it felt like a million times) already and it was the one time where enough was enough. That one day, life went dark, as if someone had turned on a switch and on came the darkness. I got home, went to the kitchen, picked up a long, sharp carving knife, took it into the living room, and sat on the floor. With tears in my eyes, I took the knife to my wrist and thought to press and pull back, that's all it would take. 'Go on, do it, take away the pain that you have' were the words in my head. But then another conversation sprung to mind; 'think how painful it would be for my parents when they arrive back from work to find their son has killed himself'. It was like a battle in my head but who would win?

Would it be the positivity or the negativity? I kept picking up the knife when the conversation in my head said, 'do it, your life is hell enough and it's time to get out of this painful, sad life.' I would then put it down once my mind thought about what Mr Newton had done, along with my parents, to get me where I was then. To know that I was not in a wheelchair was only due to their skill, support, love from my parents, and it would be a waste to let it all go in one slip of the knife. I put the knife back into the drawer away from my sights. Sadly, this moment happened a few times too many and, if I could not draw the knife on myself, then I would literally pull punches to my gut as a punishment or to say, "I'm an idiot, what am I doing?"

I thought that maybe it would be time to seek mental health help. I had conversations with my parents, telling them about how much pain I was in, and I could see my parents holding back their emotions as it was painful for them to hear what I was going through. Yet they encouraged me to say the truth and get it off my chest, so to speak. However, just opening up was not enough and, even though my parents offered their views and methods to get out from this hole, it was a deep hole. The hole was so deep and dark that I just could not climb out and could not see any positives of my life. Yet, I could put a mask on during work to be the teacher that I was being paid to be and then break down in tears later in my bedroom.

I thought about how the look of a psychiatrist's room would be, where I would be lying back on the couch, spilling the beans, saying everything that would bug me, and I would feel better. I studied the telephone directory for help and saw an advert in the local newspaper eventually which caught my eye as it was stating self-awareness. At least it was not psychiatry, which was too clinical in my mind. The lady who advertised was called Sue Gaskell. I took the courage to ring her and make an appointment.

I drove to the Derby city centre to where she rented

her place of work. I was wondering whether I would get anything out of it or whether I would go back to square one and be on the brink of suicide. I knocked on the door and the lady who opened the door exuded so much love and thoughtfulness. Sue and I sat down with a cup of tea and began conversing. I told her how it was and she summed it up in one clear phrase, that I was 'like a swan, looking so calm and beautiful in front of others but, underneath the water the swan's legs are pedalling like crazy to keep itself above water so as not to sink'. This changed my life forever, and for the better. It was like once I had said all the things which I would not dare say to my parents, like being suicidal (as it would break their hearts), they had come off my shoulders and had been shared with a lady who could take the weight. She would connect to me in the ways which I thought was not possible. She was tearful to hear the words out of my mouth, but it was a genuine love that she omitted. She gave me challenges to take home as homework to think about, which enabled me not to focus on the negatives so much but to look at the positives. It was also worked hard upon to help me in not beating myself up, both mentally and physically. On my bad days, I would be in the privacy of my bedroom and would physically punch myself in the face and body. I tried to control the punches to the body than to the face, just to prevent any questions asked. If there were bruises to the face, I would just state that I had tripped and hit my head. The hitting of my body would deflect the mental pain I had at that moment and it was uncontrollable. However, it was also more than that; it was a disliking of myself. I did not like the way I looked, so the punishment was more physical pain. Sue and I worked hard together to feel ok about the problems of what happened in the past. To take on board the painful truths about how I looked and felt about my body. To accept myself and how I looked. It was always going to be something which I was going to find hard, but having strategies on how to handle it was the way to go. The suicidal feelings of a few years ago had gone, but I wanted to improve and have rejuvenation and a love of life again like I had before all the bullying happened in my childhood.

I stayed with Sue for a number of years, which evolved to working in groups of like-minded folks. It was a pleasure to share feelings with similar people who were open and had a feeling of unconditional love, therefore it felt like a family, and to share those two hours a week was brilliant. It gave me an addictive buzz; it was like the group fed off from each other and Sue was the conductor of it all. There were times where the group were tearful, as they felt for another person who was exploring past, painful times. I was like an open book in the team, not afraid to explore feelings, which just so happen to spark off from each other. It was a safe and open place to be. I also discovered how emotions can cause illness, for example, one lady's tears of a terrible childhood cured her asthma. In other words, her asthma improved so very much the more she talked about her past and let go of pent up anger by crying. My parents were concerned for me as my demeanour had changed. I was more sparkly than before and I often spoke about the group I was with. My parents were concerned that I was involved in some kind of cult. I offered for them to join, but they declined, trusting my judgement, and they were calmed to know it's not a cult. In this period of my life, I had a go at writing an autobiography. I wrote for hours in my bedroom and my parents hardly saw me. It told of my life from an ill baby to where I was then, and my journey to that point.

I made many copies of the autobiographical book I had made in the hope that it would be published and be of an interest to many. However, it came back with very little feedback and encouragement. The copies were painful readings for my parents and close friends, but I decided to let them read it in order to know the good, the bad, and the ugly times of my life. The copies stayed in my wardrobe and just maybe I would try again, but not just yet. Maybe I could do it in more detail when more things happened in the future? That was my plan, and how it came to be.

Things were improving for the best. For example, for whatever reason, it was always difficult to say 'I love you' to my Dad and this was mentioned in the group that I went to. It was something I felt that I wanted to say but did not know how it would be and how my dad would react. I guessed that it was a manly thing that men don't say they love each other as they don't want to look weak, lovey dovey, or homosexual in any shape. The group felt that I should take the bull by the horns and introduce the idea. I started to tell my Dad I loved him when I was saying it to my Mum before going to bed, which took a lot of courage. Firstly, it was not something which my Dad could say back. Then I would try again the next evening, and the next, and so on. Eventually, the time came that Dad felt comfortable enough to say those words back to me which took the courage as I did and, ever since, we have always finished a call on the phone, and so on, with "love you". This made me warm inside, to know the connection is there. As there was not so much in terms of hugging and compliments with my dad, I guessed that maybe it was the generation that he was brought up in to not be so free with his emotions. With Sue's influence, I bought a lot of self-help books just to explore my mind, self-worth, and to tackle depression. Books written by Buddhists were also wonderful and I learnt so much from them of how to be. I discovered much later in my life that Sue Gaskell moved to New Zealand to be with her family and still keeps in contact via the internet.

Another event that happened for the best was when I was in a newsagent shop looking for my favourite magazines at the time, which was anything to do with music or photography, but that was only a ploy to see if there were any ladies being naked in any of the photographs! I was not going to be the type to buy a pornographic magazine for two reasons; 1) The top shelf was difficult to reach in the first place and I was not going to ask for assistance, and 2)

I had my pride and to buy such a dirty magazine would be highly embarrassing. I had chosen what I wanted to buy and I waited in the queue to pay for it. At that moment, a chap came in who I glanced at and then did a double-take. It was one of the three lads who went to the same Primary School who bullied me. I did not know where to go but, in those few moments, our eyes caught each other. I tried then to ignore, as I did not want to make any contact and chose to think that he was not there. The next thing I knew was the chap tapping my shoulder, and we began dialogue. It was like we were friends, as if nothing happened, and then he came out with it; he apologised for anything that happened when were children. The weight of emotion which filled my heart lessened immensely and I accepted the apology. It took a very strong character to say sorry. I was so impressed by the courage of the chap, and also gave myself a pat on the back for accepting the apology. We both wanted to admit that it was children growing up who did not know better, but now we were adults and we should move on from the past. I also learnt from Sue Gaskell of the reasons as to why children become bullies in the first place, and that was mainly because they were not getting the love and attention at home. With that emotion whirring up inside, they had to take out that aggression on someone. It's usually the child who was not good at retaliating so I, with my kind, easy-going nature, was easy, plus I was not able to catch up to the bullies. This insight as to why they did what they did put a whole new perspective in my mind and to feel sympathy for their childhood too.

Now, remember a fair few pages ago I told you that I had a good intuition and was maybe slightly clairvoyant as I felt being scared as a child in a corridor between two shops? It just so happened that, a few decades later, I met another lad called Paul in the small town of Belper, Derbyshire. This other Paul was not really known well to me but we knew each other from the chocolate factory days. We had a brief conversation and then Paul asked me for a lift so, being the kind of man I was not to say no, I proceeded to take him where he wanted. Whilst in the car, this Paul asked to borrow £20 from me (which was quite a lot of money in the 1990s) but he promised to give it back on the journey back into town. So, I took this man to a house and fifteen minutes later he came back and off again we went to town. On parking up, Paul got out and began to walk faster than me in the hope to lose me in the busy shopping area, but I did catch up to him. By then, I knew that I was not going to get my money back and that this other Paul had bought drugs with my money. I made it eventually, as swiftly as I could, to the same corridor that I remembered in my childhood. I knew that if I was to take the matter further then there will be dire consequences, so I instinctively walked away, however I was still frustrated. It knocked my trust in people, made me angry, and told me to be more cautious in future.

Chapter 13

Are You Ruud?

In 1999, I was seeing that 2000 was quickly approaching. I hoped 2000 was going to be a big year for me, and I was planning changes. I had had enough of teaching in the sense of having a regular income. It was not easy money in the first place. Saturdays were exhausting as I had non-stop classes from 9am to 6pm. I had to eat and drink whilst I listened to my pupils. Then there would be times where my lessons would be cancelled due to my pupil's ill health or, if it was nice weather, the parents would ring me with a fake cough to cancel, but I knew really that it was a time to get the barbecue out. It was uncomfortable for me when parents got too involved and pushing their children meant that I had to bite my lip to keep quiet. There was the extreme where parents would never be seen, dropping off the children and then going shopping. They never came into my studio to ask for an update on their child's development. However, I was getting rusty as I was not practicing at all on the organ. I was getting tired of playing music and listening to music, especially organ music. I was getting rusty to the point where the pupils wanted me to play and I would make a few mistakes, which was bad news for both the pupil and parents to hear. Money was not regular, plus it was not enough for a mortgage when the time came to fly from my parents' nest. I was getting itchy feet and thinking of having my own home, as I was quickly approaching my thirties.

I decided to go to the Jobcentre and see a Disabled Employment Advisor (DEA for short). This DEA was brilliant at interviewing me and asking what would be the way to go. Funnily enough, there was a job going at Ilkeston in Derbyshire to be a call centre agent for the Jobcentre. I applied, was interviewed and, a few days later, I was told I got the job. I gave the news to my music studio boss who was ok with it, and allowed my pupils to be shared amongst the other teachers.

It was a different role to the ones that I had been used to and it was a quite a distance to drive, but the environment that I was in was so comfortable and a pleasure to work in. Basically, it was taking the calls from members of the public and doing job searches on the database. It was a job which I loved, as I was helping people to change their life. If a customer rang in to do a certain job search, for example, to be a fork-lift driver and there were no vacancies at that time, I would then have a small conversation with the customer, find out their interests, previous employment details, and then try my best to match them up to other vacancies.

I would get many people complimenting me on the phone for the kindness I omitted, and the help that I gave for encouraging them. Weeks later, I would hear from the companies who advertised via the Jobcentre and they would tell me of whom they employed. When the names came out on the paper to show that I referred that customer to that job, it was a great feeling to know that I was able to help and had changed a person's life.

There were the negatives too, as with every job, I guess. I don't think there are many people out there with a job that they love completely, correct me if I am wrong? The only reason why people work is to pay the bills and to save up for the things they want to do, like go on holiday or move house and so on. The bad points of my job were that it had those customers who HAD to ring in, as they were on unemployment benefit and had an agreement to ring in weekly. Some, not all, I hasten to add, did not want a job and I could tell that they did not want a job with comments like, "I wouldn't work for that company even if they paid me three times as much", or "It's too far away to work" even though it was within a five miles radius, and so many excuses were highly transparent and tiring for me to hear. So, after hearing all the excuses under the sun, I would remark upon the comments made by the 'jobseeker' to inform the Job Centre advisor, so that they would be grilled about it when they were next in to sign for the giro cheque.

The other negative was that the role had to become customer-facing, and it happened on the occasions when other members of staff were poorly or on holiday. This is when I had to sit in the front office and help with signing giros and giving them a brief interview about their attempts in finding work. It would bring in all kinds of people into the office. Some people were really genuine, just been laid off work and adamant to get back into it before they lose their homes, and so on. However, there were also the opposite people who did not want a job at all, to show contempt at the man sitting opposite to them like I was forcing them to work a day and that it would kill them. Then there were others who made it impossible to find work due to having offensive tattoos in every place, including on their face. One moment, though, was incredibly scary. One lad, not too far off from being twenty years of age and looking like he had a drug addiction with all the fidgeting and sniffing he did, sat in front of me stating that he wanted his giro cheque early. I asked my manager if this would be possible, but the man was not allowed to have it early because he had already had so many early payments and there was a limit. I gave him the bad news that he did not want to hear, and I certainly did not fancy giving it him either. The next thing to go off was shouting abuse at me, and it escalated to him pulling a hammer out from under his jacket. I immediately pressed the panic alarm under my desk. Out came Bob. Bob was a Jobcentre advisor; a Scottish chap who was an ex-naval officer. Bob rushed to my desk and this lad jumped out of his seat and fled outside with Bob hot on his trail. The police continued the chase and Bob came back into the office to make sure I was ok. Bob was hard as nails but also had a heart of gold. I could never grasp half of the conversation with Bob's thick Scottish accent, but I got the general gist.

Although one incident hit me hard as I, with other members of staff, were reprimanded for using the database to look for a person who had hit the news as an accomplice to murder. It was a magnet; once one person saw the records then so many more followed.

These people were warned separately in the office that an inquiry would be taken place and then what actions to be taken would follow later. It was a time where I, with the others, was worried about our jobs and futures. The action taken was a warning, and that stayed on my records for ten years, which was a huge lesson to learn. The lesson to learn was to take data protection seriously from then onwards.

So, back to the positives. The salary was regular, I had a good work pension, and I met great colleagues who started to nickname me as 'Ruud' because I looked a little like the footballer Ruud van Nistelrooy. I wished that I had Ruud's money but saw that, facially, they had a point. From the neck down, the similarity stopped! The idea of being a lookalike as a sideliner was not going to happen. In the workplace, there was plenty of banter, even amongst management. For example, the manager and the deputy played around with a fake toy hand. The supervisor could be on the phone when, all of a sudden, she would feel this cold hand on her shoulder. Yes, she wanted to scream but at same time she needed to be professional, and the laughter in the office made it worse as, by then, she had realised the prank. Revenge would then be on the cards. The deputy would not expect revenge and, when on the phone, the swivel office seat would suddenly be toyed with, twirled, the height would go from high to low, and then reclined. Whilst this revenge was going on, the professionalism was kept amazingly on the phone. This gave a sense of freedom for the other employees to do similar with each other.

I did not really wish to build up close friendships too much in the Jobcentre, as I had three great pals in my life and they were Dave, Lee, and Mark. Whilst working in the Jobcentre, I was informed that, in one year, I was the best colleague in Derbyshire to get the most people into work. This stunned me and I felt it was something that I was getting pleasure out of. It was the right time to find a home, as it was getting late in the year 2000 and I had promised to myself that I wanted a place of my own before the year 2000 ended. I felt like I had overstayed my welcome at my parents' house, however not in any way that they showed they wanted me out. In fact, quite the opposite, and it was a sad day when I announced that I was looking for somewhere else. I wanted a place of my own for many different reasons, one of them being that my age of 28 felt like I was living as a Mummy's boy, and this was not the feeling I wanted to have for myself. I thought it would be an investment to be on the property ladder and IF the time came that I was able to date a young lady, it would be freer to have my own bachelor pad. After searching for a property for a few weeks, I visited a couple of maisonettes, but my Dad gave advice that it's like a flat and if the person above has a leak, it gets difficult to sort out. Plus, the sharing of a garden would not be so comfortable, so I declined such properties, and then my Mum saw it! The property in the newspaper was in Oakwood in Derby and was a one bedroom semi-detached house in a nice area at a reasonable price.

I fell in love with the property immediately as I went around it. Even though it was small with one bedroom, it was easy to maintain, easy to get to work, with nice neighbours, and in a quiet location. The living room had a kitchen in the same room, with just a half wall between them. It had a small rectangular garden with a little patio and a drive to park my car; everything was perfect. I placed an offer with the estate agents where they advised that another person had placed the same bid. However, the owner was in the estate agency themselves and liked me enough to take my offer. Weeks passed while the lawyers did what they had to do to make the contracts work, and then I was given a final date for when the papers could be signed. It was close to Christmas of 2000, but I did have the keys in that year as I wished for. My parents and I went around different companies for furniture, and we bought a sofa, a chair, and then a posh-looking glass dining table with chairs. Mum had so much stuff in the house that was duplicated, that I could take without having to re-buy. Mum gave me things like a duvet, bed clothes, knives and forks, plus much more, so that I was ready to move in on the Friday just before Christmas. I put up decorations for the festive season and it looked amateurish, yet cute. There was a moment of my life where I sat in the living room on the Saturday, and it was a realisation that the wall in front was mine, the ceiling was mine, the stairs to the left were mine.... Then, I shouted "YES!" I accidentally just blurted it out, so I then shouted "SORRY" for my neighbours. It was one of the greatest feelings in my life. Needless to say, I came over to visit for Christmas time at my parents'. It did not mean that it was the end of the connection with me. Mum was heartbroken somewhat to have both sons that had fled the nest, but she realised it was my time to fly. Plus, my Mum would always take me back if it did not work out for me as her love was always unconditional.

The house became a home even more so when I invited my pal, Dave, to view it for the first time. Dave remarked upon it by saying, "So this is Northers' Nest!" The name stuck, and the next thing was my Dad talking to a local potter, asking him to make a clay plaque to be put up outside the door. This was made within weeks and it said 'Northers' Nest' with a picture of a nest and chicks whistling a tune underneath. My house felt like home and it was perfect. It was a feeling of freedom. To come and go with no questions asked, and only myself to deal with.

Once this honeymoon of freedom settled, an aspect of

boredom came into play. I could visit my parents at any time and I could call them at any time. Yet I wanted to show that I could fend for myself, and I wanted to show that I was able to do all the things like shopping, cleaning, and any other chores. The things I could not do were things like mowing the lawn, to which my parents came over regularly to do in the spring and summer. Later on, one neighbour saw what was going on and he offered to help by taking on the gardening for me. I was overcome by his generosity that I treated the chap with a bottle of something at every Christmas for all his work. Plus, a funny coincidence occurred when I had post addressed to Mr and Mrs P. Northridge. Funny, I thought to myself, that I could have gotten so drunk one night and married a complete stranger?! But, as it turned out, my next door neighbour was another Paul Northridge; how coincidental was that? So, with the post in my hands, I went next door and introduced myself as Paul Northridge, to which the neighbour thought it was highly unlikely and that I was an absolute fruitcake, but when post arrived to my neighbour by error also, then it was confirmed as true!

Going back to the boredom and the freedom of being at 'Northers Nest' meant something wrong was happening. I was drinking too much alcohol. It began slowly by just being at weekends to being every other evening to then every night. The problem was that I was getting addicted to drink, and it was controlling me. I would drink for anything that happened which caused a reflex to drink; I disguised the reason to drink because I had a bad day or to celebrate because it was a good day. I would drink only for the point to be drunk, to be out, and to be away from myself and my resentful feelings again. I was surprised that feelings of negativity came back but I numbed it with alcohol. It was due to the fact that I was thinking I was a failure in the sense of being single still and not the man I wanted to be. I was destroying myself. It was feelings that I could not stop drinking; I even hid it from all my friends and family. I would report in to my parents by ringing them after work, which meant that all evening was free to drink. I was increasing in weight, and I had many attempts to stop drinking with different tactics. I decided to get a hobby. I bought an organ (of great expense) from my mate Dave, from the place he worked at as a music sales assistant. The ploy worked for a while, as it helped to get my fingers tapping again, because dust had settled on my musical skills by then. However, the dust on the organ gathered within a short period of time, and the organ stool became a small table to put food and drinks on.

I then went on a self-help CD from a famous American self-help guru. It was enlightening and, again, it helped for a longer period, but a moment in my life just sparked fury where children in a shop made fun of me and I went straight over to the wine and beer department. The CD just stayed in my collection and was never used again until it was car-booted not long after. I had the excuse that self-help CDs were designed for able-bodied people as it was showing that daily exercise would increase my energy and love of life, but I did not love life. Also, I was lying to myself; I could have exercised, I could have gone swimming, or I could have gone to the local gym, but I was not interested in myself or my future.

I had an urge to help people in my life, wanting to help people to make the changes that they wished for, and so I took up a course in Person-Centred Counselling. The first year was brilliant and I passed with the equivalent of an A-Level. The down sides of people knowing that someone is a counsellor or training to be one is that when a typical conversation goes off, the other person suspects that counselling techniques are being used. They then close their books to say about their problems! Or, you can mention to a person at a party that you're a counsellor, and the floodgates would open up so that person can tell their whole life story.

Like most people in the counselling class, I wished to move on and go towards the diploma next. It was a long process and mind-delving, exploring own issues and deep-centred issues. There was plenty of practice counselling between each other and I learnt a lot with the group. There were many remarks that people felt so comfortable to be able to open up to me and I could take anything that they wished to explore. Plus, I had to have at least fifteen professional counsellor sessions, which links quite nicely to the next part.

First of all, I could not track down Sue Gaskell who had helped me so much before. The counsellor that I eventually found was brilliant to share my feelings of drinking, thoughts about me being single, and issues with trust as per the small story of the man taking £20 off me which broke a lot of trust in people. The period of counselling happened for over a year but it was not working, even though I explored these things, yet I was suicidal again and drink as a way of killing me was a way of doing it slowly but not so obvious as a knife to the wrist or a jump from a cliff, etc. Painfully to say it, it was true I wanted to die. Life was not too bad, as I kept exploring in my counselling sessions. I went over the facts that I had my own house, I had a job that I loved, had parents who loved me dearly, had great friends, but yet I was not truly happy. I was really thinking that this approach of counselling was not working for me, and that I was wondering if I beyond help. The diploma in counselling did not go as planned for reasons of the following. The first point was that I was thinking whether counselling really works. The second point was that I was drinking too much and could barely get the coursework done to the standard it needed to be. Lastly, a teacher who came to teach for the last season was difficult to be with. It was difficult to put the finger on what was making students uncomfortable with him but it was there, including myself having this same feeling. In a counselling environment of trying to be open and learn, it was not good, to say the least, for most of the class. This meant that I never gave work in as there had to be written stuff of a personal nature, but I felt that I could not trust the teacher with that information.

With that, a few other students did not pass either and I really thought that it was time I moved on from this stage in my life. I really thought so negative about counselling that it would be not great to work as a counsellor.

Now, I forgot to mention that I had a love of writing poems. I would have evenings off from alcohol to vent my thoughts and anger by putting pen to paper. I was not a scholar and never wanted to be a talented writer but, by this time in my life, I dreamed of being richer, like most of the population do, and thought that would help the depression. Maybe I would not only write poems on how I felt, but maybe I would write the lyrics to a Christmas song and then I would be rich as it would be sold all over the world. My poems were basically what you see is what you get. There was nothing cryptic about my poems, and I disliked how people boasted about how intelligent they were by writing poems of an obscure nature then having people studying their work. For example, you could write a line of anything; the cow was blue with joyful delight, but that would confuse people and then they would look behind the meaning of it all. Maybe the cow was not really a cow; maybe it was a metaphor for the poet's next door neighbour who had a blue door, and so on! The same went for modern art, where they would have a coat hanger on a stick with a traffic cone and the artist would explain the concept of it all, such as it being about how people struggle with life. Really it's just junk with an explanation behind it! Yet they would sell the junk for millions of pounds. Amazeballs! The very same happened with a blank canvas apart from a black square which sold for millions. Now, to me, that would probably be worth £10, so I think it's just people jumping on the bandwagon.

I wrote so many pads-worth of poems with mainly angst. It was about how I felt about being single, my body, and my thoughts about a negative future. It would make Morrisey feel sorry for me, I could guess. At times, I would read them back as it was if it was not really me writing the words, and it had just blurted out of my emotions. It would surprise both me and those who dared to read them how dark they really were, especially when I portrayed myself to others as a light-hearted and easy-going chap. Maybe if this book takes off, I will release another book entitled 'My Poems'.

Chapter 14

One Wedding And Funeral

Let me diverge slightly, back to my employment. I loved my job in the Jobcentre; it was inspiring for me, as I mentioned already. It gave me reasons to get out of bed in the mornings and ready to make a change for others, but I could not change my own direction. However, the manager (the one with the joke hand) one day gave sad news to the organisation that the team which I was on was no longer going to be at Ilkeston, and it was being moved to Derby city centre. Sad news indeed, as I loved the team so much that I worked with. The team had a young, vibrant feel to it and was steered by the manager, Sheena, who shone like a star. She was very easy-going, yet people did not abuse her nice nature, apart from the usual office pranks. However, it was time to move on, and the new manager from Derby, Mary, visited the team and was immediately impressed by the staff there. She asked me personally if I would like to be the Deputy Supervisor. Of course, I could not turn down the offer as I was good at my job; I would be the main member of staff who would train new colleagues. I was hitting the targets and more so. The warmth I exuded to the customers was naturally encouraging to the staff I worked with and the customers I looked after. By the way, I had a rapport with one customer by telephone who also had a disability and he really wanted to work for the Jobcentre. I advised that I would case study him, which meant that the chap did not have to ring in so often, and that I would look regularly on his behalf. Surely enough, one day, a vacancy became available and I passed the information on to this chap. I was to learn that the chap had got the job. I was well chuffed and I hoped the chap was too.

That short story was important to know about because, on the first day in my new role in Derby Jobcentre, I was approached by a chap who shook my hand and said who he was. He described that I got him the place in the Jobcentre and gave me great comments on my customer service skills. It was a delight to meet up and show mutual respect for one another.

The role that I had was pretty much the same as what I was doing already; training new members of staff, answering the phones, and doing job searches. However, there was more to my role, being an Assistant Supervisor. I had to draw up rotas for break times to make sure there were enough phone lines covered, I had to make up reports, and I had to draw statistics up, which was not my cup of tea. There were days when the Supervisor was off poorly and I stepped up as Acting Supervisor. This meant going into managerial meetings, holding my own team meetings, and this also meant that the focus was on me which was uncomfortable, as I did not look for attention. I had times when customers were not happy with their experience of talking to a fellow colleague so calls were escalated to me, and that meant a lot of negotiation with apologies. The role was challenging at times, but I held onto the post very well and it was a possibility that I would be the Supervisor one day, or so I thought.

During this time of working in the Jobcentre, I must tell you things that went off in my personal life. Ashley, my brother, got married to Anette in Spain, where my parents and I flew over to be there to celebrate this huge occasion. We were there only a few years before in Spain to celebrate Ashley and Anette's 30th birthdays, as they are only a few days apart from each other. After the partying and the sore heads, there was another reason to celebrate; they got engaged a few days into that holiday.

Time went by while organising the wedding, and the big day came. I had prepared a best man's speech, as I was honoured to be by my brother's side on the big day. It was a typically hot Spanish day with a blue sky, and I had taken a fair bit of time to work on my speech for my brother next to the swimming pool. Let me go off- track a bit more to fill you in about Ashley and his wife-to-be. Ashley was a golfer, and a professional one at that. He worked in a local golf course, learning the trade of how to make the pro-shop work. He learned about becoming a golf teacher and built up a large clientele. Ashley became well-known and rubbed shoulders with many keen golfers. One day, he got head-hunted to work at Royal Mid-Surrey, and then later to Wentworth, which are all posh golf courses. During this time, Ashley, on an evening out, spotted a lady touring London, and they caught each other's eye. They made conversation and, before they knew it, they became boyfriend and girlfriend over a period of dating in each other's home countries, as Anette was German. They eventually thought that the dating had gone well and wanted to make a go of living together. They decided to go to a neutral country, and so Spain was the place to be. Ashley found a job there and a home to live in, so they both landed in the warm climate of Spain, but the job that Ashley was promised collapsed. However, Anette was able to land an estate agent role in a short period of time until Ashley began working as a manger of a golf shop. Anyway, back on track of the wedding day. The wedding was funny somewhat, as Anette's Mum was a music teacher and she was playing the music for the big day. However, being a German lady, she did not know the music chosen very well and the order they should go in. When it was Anette's time to walk down the aisle, it was with a typical classical piece of music, but not the wedding march as planned. The priest then said a few words, and our Mum had to do a reading from the gospel. Getting from her seat to the podium was accompanied by Anette's Mum on the organ, and it was the traditional Wedding March. There was a little chuckle from the congregation in the church, and Mum had to stand at the podium until this long piece of music was over.

The wedding reception was lovely, as there was a buffet with champagne, but there was one big problem; flies. Flies had swarmed this outside buffet, with flies on the food and flies landing in people's drinks. It just happened on this day that it was a swarm that would not leave. Anette's half-brother, not much older than 14, took out his trumpet to serenade the married couple but, in a strange twist, moments later, he ran into a patio door. It was like a scene from 'You've Been Framed', where the person did not notice the glass and then wallop, he ends up on the floor. It was not a comical moment though once we saw the blood on his face. He was as fine as he could be moments later and the drinks, plus flies, kept flowing.

People gradually left to change clothes at their villas and to prepare for the evening event. I had rehearsed my speech with Anette's sister, Stephanie, as it had to be translated into German due to half of the guests invited being such. They planned everything to a tee, pardon the golf pun. The night went so well, with lovely food, music, and company, although I could not relax and didn't want to drink too much as I has difficulty getting my words out at the best of times but, when drunk, I just had glossy eyes and a warm smile, without a chance to speak. I avoided the alcohol until my speech was over. The main course was over, and now to the speeches. It was great, as our Dad did an improvised speech and it was from the heart, stating he knew that Anette and Ashley were meant to be. There were a few more speeches from Ashley, followed by Ashley's Father-in-Law. However, the time came for the spotlight to be turned onto me. I could not stand for a long period of time but, I hasten to add, I was great at improvising with what was around me. I placed my right knee on the chair and held the rest by my hands on the table, with my left leg keeping me upright as I stood to do the speech. I reflected on the times of being together as brothers and all the things we did, but I went off-course with a risk of telling Anette about Ashley's first love. I described a soft, kind, loving character that flew all these miles to Spain for the occasion and pulled out Ashley's first cuddly toy which our parents kept in the attic for all those years. Ashley embraced Banji, as he called it, and he was really happy for the warm, funny speech from his brother. Then, once the desserts were eaten, it was time to party and dance. It was a night of fun, drinking, plus an opportunity to engage with both sides of the family. To be honest, I relaxed too much through alcohol and regretted it deeply with an extremely sore head the next day.

One small story to state is that, during the wedding week, we had a celebratory family-and-friends meal, but I can't recall if it was before or after the wedding. It was an evening time where we all sat outside enjoying time together when suddenly, a praying mantis just landed on the table in front of me. The ladies all screamed and hid where they could, whilst I just stared at this unusual creature. Yes, I had seen one during a wildlife documentary, but not in real life. It felt like it was looking at me and the other guests, and it stayed - not in any way nervous - for a good few minutes to then vanish into the evening sky. It almost felt like an alien came to visit to say hello, and then went back to its planet.

Since Ashley and Anette have been married, they had a daughter, Lea, and a son, Ben. The family moved from Spain to Madeira, then back to Spain, and later moved to Canada to follow Ashley's golf career. I hasten to add that the Madeiran white port is awesome, which I sampled once too often.

Now, if you remember a while ago, I mentioned John, who worked with me at the chocolate factory. Sorry, but I have this habit of jumping around on this story. John really moved on from friendship to spend more time with his girlfriend, Monica, as they met in the factory and fell in love. John did mention that, during the time when my Mum had cancer, he had recovered from nose cancer. I was unsure if that was the truth or not as John had a dry sense of humour, until he said that he was really ill with it but now he is fine as he had been free from it for a few years. Time went by and I had lost contact with John, although I thought about him a lot, and this was at a time before Facebook existed. It was a surprise for me when I was told to ring Monica one evening as she had tried to ring me at my parent's home, but I was living at 'Norther's Nest' by now. I rang Monica to catch up and to ask about John when she mentioned that he had cancer again, but this time it was terminal. It saddened me to hear this news, of course, and I wanted to meet with John before he passed away. I made several visits to their home and it was sad to see a man I once knew as fit and athletic-looking reduced to a shell of skin and bones. Yet John still had his humour. He was finding it hard to talk, but I could see how happy he was to see me. In such situations, I had a good sense of humour, as I would lighten the atmosphere. I remarked on the days of when we worked together and the times when the belt was too fast for us all to catch up on. I could only see the top of John's head behind all the boxes of chocolates. John never ever really laughed, just chuckled internally with a nice smile, but when he chuckled, his shoulders would uncontrollably shake, and that's what John did in that living room, on the sofa, with lots of cushions around him. It was a pleasure for me to see and remember him by; he was an ill chap, but still able to chuckle.

A few days later, I brought a computer console for us to play together which entertained John for a few hours every day, and I was able to see him four days before he got really sick. It wasn't long, though, as John lost his fight and, on the day of the funeral, Marky and I performed a piece of music in the church. I also did a small speech filled with fond memories of working with John. However, I was very nervous and upset, so it was not to the standard I wanted it to be.

Chapter 15

Lee And His Best Men

Another thing that happened in the Jobcentre years was that Lee, the friend of mine who is an entertainer, moved around to different hotels and caravan sites for changes of scenery or different types of work. During Lee's career in a hotel in Cirencester, he met a young waitress called Kate. Kate was on a working Visa from Russia and they became friends. They later became partners but her Visa expired, and so they dated by travelling to each other's countries. During this time of their courtship, Kate's Mum suggested a lady by the name of Yulia (an old college friend of Kate's) who she thought would be perfect for me and so I had her email address to correspond with. Although it was not something that I had thought about, it was going to be a potential relationship. Craftily, Kate told Yulia that I wanted to learn Russian and about the Russian culture. I was told the same; that Yulia wanted to learn English. I thought it would be just to learn each other's language and that at least it was a bit of a hobby as I loved to write, so it was not difficult. Yulia had had a bad time in her life in regards to the opposite sex and really was not intending this correspondence to become a relationship. I felt the same way as I was, by then, fed up with dating.

The communication was basic stuff really, about the weather and learning about each other's cultures. I was single and, for all I knew, she was too, but it was highly unlikely to be seen as a possible romance for a few good reasons. One) I deemed myself, at that moment in my life, as undateable, and that's another word to go into the dictionary. Two) Russia was a million miles away in my mind. Three) she was a single Mum and, at that time in my life, I was not sure if I was ready to be a Step-Dad. The fourth and final point was that I knew that Yulia did not know English very well, as Kate was back in Russia to help her write and translate. For about a year and a half, Yulia and I wrote to each other with both of us not thinking of it as a relationship and just to have an interest as a pen pal for each other. Going back in time when I met Wayne Anthony, the clairvoyant, he did say I would get married and would have a strong connection to Russia, but I shelved that memory.

Lee and Kate planned their wedding in Russia. I was chosen to be one of the two best men, as Lee had another good friend, Roger, who worked with Lee in the entertainment of tourists. The plans were all set, everyone had their Visas, plane tickets, and away we went. When I arrived in the airport, the Russian staff of the female kind was gorgeous and the ladies on security were not butch in any way. Boy, this was one time I did not mind being frisked! I thought I would say I had a loaded weapon down my trousers but I did not want to end up in a Russian prison on the first day there! The journey on the coach was a rocky one as there are many long, bumpy roads with potholes everywhere. It was apparent, straight away, that Russian drivers were extreme and had no etiquette as they hardly indicated and had no gestures to each other of who will go out first and it became more like who had the fastest car or who is least afraid of dying. It was a winter wedding for the couple and, to be brutally honest, Russian winter is cruel with extreme minus temperatures. Most of the houses looked dilapidated and I wondered if anyone lived in them. There were lots of apartment blocks, more than houses it seemed, but I was not counting. There was one stop before people got to their homes and the chance to stretch their legs. It was a chance to use the gas station's toilet, and the English visitors were in for a shock as the toilet was like a small wooden shack with a hole in the floor to do their business in. I refrained from this toilet opportunity and held it in until we got to our destination. Once arriving at a block of flats, Roger and I noticed that the flat had a bit of a retro feeling inside as there were video players being used still in people's homes. Outside, on the roads, the cars were old-looking with mainly Skoda being the main choice of most folks there, and fumes came out which did not smell of petrol or diesel but more like gas, which concerned me.

The food that Roger and I ate was very basic, like salami, bread, and soups. I felt somewhat amazed with how poor people were, but generally happy. There were excursions to different places of Tula, which is south of Moscow, and then one trip to Moscow itself, which was amazing. There was a lot of snow about, naturally, but, in Moscow, they had cleared the pavements more so. The long walks around places such as the Kremlin and Red Square were beautiful, and to have a photo to show that I had made it to Moscow was a tremendous feeling, but I was missing my woolly hat, which was accidentally left on the coach. The photo was funny, as it was me in Red Square smiling through gritted teeth, almost saying to the cameraman, "Just hurry up, will you!" Well, anyone would, as it was minus twenty-five that day! It was an amazing feeling, though, to stand in Red Square, viewing the Kremlin and, even though I was not politically-minded or interested in history, it was visually awesome.

Lee and Kate took me over to meet Yulia for the first time. I was nervous as I knew very little of the Russian language, and Yulia did not know much English either. It was helpful for Kate to translate, and we had very basic conversations with nothing at all in-depth being said. It was somewhat concerning to meet Yulia's brother, as he was an ex-military chap who had served in the Chechen war and he had a gleam in his eyes, which was a bit unnerving. Then, there was Grandma who was bed bound in the flat, and I also met Yulia's parents, who were warm and could not do enough for my time in their home. I was then introduced to Yulia's daughter, Anya; a baby who was only six months old and fast asleep in her cot. The food and company was great but still, Yulia and I were seeing it all as nothing but friendship.

A few days into the holidays came Lee and Kate's wedding. Now, I must say, the Russians know how to celebrate a wedding and it puts the English weddings to shame, to some extent. The first part of a typical wedding was that Lee and Kate slept in different flats the night before, nothing new there, right? But, in the morning of the big day, Lee had to travel in a car decorated with bows and ribbons. Lee, with his best men beside him, walked to her residence, of course, in their suit and ties. Lee, approaching the building, notices Yulia and a man at the entrance with a decorated door. People who knew the couple, and onlookers, gathered around as Lee got closer. So the games now began. With the help of translators on-site, Lee had to get into the building and up the stairs gradually by answering questions. The questions were all related to Kate, like her date of birth or her parents' dates of birth. There was a twist to this game as, if Lee got any answers wrong, he had to pay coins to Kate, so it made it fun for all to see how well he knew his future wife. Eventually, Lee and everyone else made it to Kate's flat with a few coins removed from his pocket. For the last game, there was a balloon on the flat door which Lee had to hit with a dart, thus releasing a key from inside the balloon. It took a few goes but it popped in the end, and there he met his wife in her wedding dress. There was food and drink spread out on the tables for all and later, we made our way to the Kremlin (church) for the actual ceremony. Yulia, being Kate's bridesmaid, had more of a role in this as she stood by her side and held a crown above Kate's head for a long period of time. I felt sorry for her at this moment, as it must have been at least twenty minutes. There was a lot of Russian singing by the priest of the Kremlin which was all confusing to me and the rest of the English people there. Once that ceremony was over, it was time to do more games and traditions.

Lee and Kate had to be driven over seven bridges as a good luck sign and, once at the seventh bridge, Lee had to carry Kate over that bridge without dropping her. Now, there was plenty of snow and ice therefore it was a bit unfair, but it was a challenge that Lee took on. Why could we not have married in July? Lee was probably thinking. It was a long bridge and the rules were that Lee could use his best men to help to carry. That was ok for Roger, one of the best men, but I had no chance, so Lee chose another chap to take my role on this occasion. It needs to be mentioned that if the bride was to be dropped at any moment, it meant the marriage was doomed, arrrrrgh! I was relieved that I was not able to carry Kate, as I did not want to be the doom-bearer of the marriage! When the evening came for food, drink, and dance, Yulia and I sat together throughout the evening until it was time to dance, which the Russians just loved to do. It's not like the English way at all, where you just have kids running around on the empty dancefloor. After a few more drinks, people would have the courage to get up and look for others to join them. The Russian style is that it's a free-for-all to get on the dancefloor first. It's packed solidly with dancers; men don't look embarrassed to dance, unlike most of the English men who look like they are dancing on hot coals.

During that wedding party night, conversation between Yulia and I was very difficult, but we tried to learn each other's language a bit more and talking improved as the wine flowed. Lee and Roger performed together on stage, which brought memories back for me of when I saw them in Mablethorpe. Roger and Lee performed Rock 'n' Roll hits to the more modern stuff of Elton John. Lee then performed solo with his ukulele, singing songs of George Formby. The Russians, who had never seen them play before, were amazed and enjoyed this selection of English music. Then, it was back to the disco where everybody danced, including the English guests. Yulia was on the dancefloor for a while and, to be honest, I did not mind, as she looked so happy. I sat watching everyone having fun when I caught a Russian couple's eyes. They looked at each other and spoke, and then came to talk to me. They spoke very good English and said, 'We wanted to say to you that you've been touched by God'. They explained that my eyes were the windows to my soul, and they felt that connection. I thanked them, although I did not know how to take it, but I have gotten a few people saying that I have something special about me. Once the wedding was over and we all flew back home, normality hit. It was back to work, and it was not where I wanted to be, as you will read next.

After almost a year and half in the new role as Deputy in the Jobcentre, the news came into the office that the call centre was being shut down and moved to a much larger building in Lincolnshire. I had the choice to stay where I was and take on another role, or to move to Lincolnshire. There was no question about it; even though the job was lovely, to move away would mean being away from my parents who helped so much, and be away from my mates would be changing my life for the worse. So, it was time to find another role in the Jobcentre, and the first role I had was trying to encourage those who had been out of work for a while with ill health to join in with a new government incentive. This incentive meant they can get a cash bonus if they began to work, even in part-time employment, and come off incapacity benefit.

The conversation that I experienced would go a little like this;

"Hello." A man's voice would answer the phone.

"Hi, is that Mr Smith?" I would ask positively.

"Yes it is, who is that?" They would answer with the same amount of positivity in their voice as to match mine, although they would be concerned if it was any telesales going on. We know how much we love being cold called, don't we?

"It's Paul from the Jobcentre..."

"Oh." A disappointed tone was heard, and I continued.

"Did you know that if you take up a job, be it part-time or more, then the government would give you a cash bonus..."

"I'll stop you there, son." A harsh and ill tone of voice travelled into my earpiece. "I am not well enough for any work, and how dare you ring me up when you know that have the symptoms of..." They would then list the issues that they have and terminate the call before I could say another word. There were also other people who were up for an argument with me, and that's where I would have to terminate the call.

I thought that I, too, was classed as disabled, but I did not class myself as unable to do anything because I could do something. I could sit and I could talk, so therefore I was able. It took a fair bit of control at times not to say what I really felt to certain customers on the phone. In my mind, I would criticise depressed people, being there myself on one too many occasions, but the only thing to do was to pick myself up and not to dwell on the negatives. I would think of those that I spoke to with bad backs and then compare my body to theirs. I had a bad back forever, and yet I guess they were still sitting and speaking to me. The question of, "Why don't you do call centre work like me?" came into my mind, and I had to fight back that sentence so very often or be out of work myself! This job lasted about a few months, after which I had to say my mind to a manager, as it was a job that nobody should endure due to it being just full of negativity. The next role I had was creating jobs on to the system by going out to companies and asking if they wanted to advertise their vacancies via the Jobcentre. Some managers were positive, but then there were some would respond by saying they get only those who are just applying because they are forced to and that it's therefore a waste of time. Then, it was chasing up if the post was filled and finding out whether it was via the Jobcentre advertisement. That, too, was ok, but it was not fulfilling my feelings. It did not have enough customer engagement, so I had itchy feet and began to look elsewhere for work.

I began writing CVs, sending out application forms, and sometimes hearing back a negative response but often hearing nothing at all, which I thought it was rude. I then saw a post for a call centre for a company that ships out new kitchens and bathrooms to their customers. I sent an application form, was asked for an interview, and got the job. It was two full days of training, where some of the information went way over my head. The other people in my group were getting it all or so it seemed. Like in school, I was always afraid or ashamed to put up my hand to say, 'I don't get it!' so I joined the rest of the huge call centre with small teams of about 6 groups, and was set up to talk to customers. There were good calls that I answered to book in dates of deliveries to customers' homes. Then there were the bad calls, where items were wrongly delivered or broken and it delayed the fitting of the customer's kitchen. These calls were mainly heated, involved a lot of the customers swearing down the phone, and then got escalated to a supervisor. If we were unable to resolve the complaint, then it went to another team in the organisation. The job was basically call after call after call. The phone hardly stopped ringing and the call board showed of a long waiting time for customers to get through. That thirty minutes of waiting to speak with me did not help the customer's emotion in any shape, and just added more fuel to their fire.

The whole call centre was situated in an ex-prison unit, and I had to park my car a fair distance to the building, but the bosses did allow me the nearest place possible to help. By then, I had to use crutches permanently to get around which helped so much. I had to wear a hi-vis vest for safety, as there was a lot of business happening; trucks with deliveries went out from the centre, and there were so many warehouse staff with fork-lift trucks zooming by. There were many security chaps on-site also to make sure no-one was stealing any of the items, which was happening a fair bit and so people were fired on the spot.

The shifts were early morning, weekends, and evenings, so it was hard on my personal life. The work was very stressful, especially when deliveries, for whatever reason, were not going to be delivered that day to customers then I, with the rest of the team, had to call these very unhappy customers with the bad news. I began, again, looking for another job. However, I must also advise that my alcohol addiction escalated in this period of my life, as I was feeling unsuccessful in love and was also spending most of my days in a job which I hated, getting very little connection with others in the call centre and with the customers on the phone. Plus, the phone calls were depressing mainly and, to calm down in the evenings, I would hit the bottle. The type of drink did not really matter to me; it could be wine, beer, or spirit, anything which had a strong percentage. Often, I would spend my evenings drinking and watching the television. Before I knew it, it was three o'clock in the morning and I slept with drink all over the floor from which I spilled over the carpet. The next day, I would have a pounding head and tell myself that that was the last time. It was not doing anything good for my health, as I had added so much weight on at this period of my life. The GP recognised the gaining of weight, and monitored my high levels of blood pressure and cholesterol. Eventually, I was given tablets to take for 'ailments'. I thought I had let both myself and my body down, so the negative cycle rolled around. I often reflected on the near-death experience I had at fourteen years of age and that I was causing serious damage to my body. Even this reflecting did not help, and I was on a mission again to have a slow death by alcohol.

Chapter 16

Long Distance Love

In one night of debauchery, I must have had the usual of too much to drink and fell asleep next to the heater. With not being able to feel my right foot at all, I must have caught it on the heater or kept it too near because, days later, I was walking around my home and noticed blood markings on the carpet. I went over to ask my Mum to have a look, as I was unable to see underneath. My Mum said immediately that it needed to be seen by the GP, where they gave me antibiotics. It did not clear up at all in the five days. I was feeling terribly ill, and so a visit was arranged to hospital for a specialist. The specialist saw me and said that I would need treatment. I thought it would be a visit in the next few days for an hour or so and then leave. It was a shock to the system when the doctor advised that I had to stay in from now! Mum had to leave me in a ward and get my things. The doctors put me on an intravenous drip of antibiotics and monitored me regularly, as it was questionable if the lower limb could be gangrenous. It was a worrying time for all, to say the least, and, after five days in hospital, I was free to leave, but with regular visits to the local surgery for check-ups and dressing changes. I thought to myself that changes had to happen.

I knew that I was overweight, and I knew that I was on the road to a long, slow, painful death. Truthfully, there were visions in my head that I did not like and could not escape from. I reflected on the near-death experience, again, which I had at fourteen years old, and it related to where I was feeling now. I will be brutally honest; I saw a vision of myself hanging in the kitchen from a tie from the open staircase. At fourteen years of age, I could not relate to it, and thought it may be visions of another person. But now, as an adult, that memory flooded back, and the feelings of where I was now matched up to what I felt at fourteen. I thought long and hard. I wanted to make the change. The first thing was to find somewhere new to live, as the vision in my head of myself hanging was that of where I was living currently. Perhaps if I lived somewhere else, it may give me new feelings. Like a fresh start in life. I saw one property that was literally two bungalows away from my mate Marky who, by then, had divorced his wife and moved back with his Mum. It was a perfect bungalow and I tried my hardest to sell my home. There were no takers, apart from those who gave a ridiculous asking price for it. Eventually, the bungalow got sold to another person and that was that. So, another point entered my mind. I had been saving up money and, for what, to move to another house? But that was not working, so I took it off the market and thought about travelling. I had already travelled to see my brother a fair few times in Spain and Madeira as Ashley worked in those countries in that period. I had still kept in touch with Yulia in Russia by emailing at least weekly. I thought to myself that it was nearly two years after Lee's wedding and it was about time to catch up with my pen pal.

Yulia and I organised the Visa and flights and, this time, it was going to be in September so not a wintery visit. I was happy about a summery visit, as I had a few bruises on my arse from sliding around in Tula during Lee and Kate's wedding. I heard from Lee that Yulia had, by this time, a boyfriend, and that was not bothering me, as it was mentioned a few times that we had a pen pal friendship and nothing more. I also understood, from Yulia's letters, that she had been learning more English and that maybe we wouldn't need a translator so much, unlike me, who probably learnt about twenty words in Russian. So, my holiday was set up with invitation and Visa done. It's not an easy place to visit as to apply for Visa meant providing my bank details and proving that I have been invited by friends. I flew to Russia all by myself with a translation book in my pocket just in case I got stuck in the airport. Although my skill in pronouncing Russian was poor, I was just going to point at the Russian sentence that I wanted to say; well, that was my plan, anyway. Once landed in Moscow, I was excited for the possibility of those lovely security ladies frisking me but it all ran smoothly, sad but true. Maybe singing Elton John's 'Nikita' as loud as possible could get me restrained? Yulia's parents were waiting in the arrivals section of the airport with a taller two year old Anya; she was no longer that little baby girl I saw on the first visit. She was a smiling little girl, and I made her giggle from the expressions on my face. One question though; where was Yulia? Yulia's Mum described the best she could that she was working and that she would meet me at the flat later.

The journey was two hours in the car, with all the possible pleasantries said, and I was tired of the travelling. Calm came into the car for the rest of the journey even though Yulia's parents hardly spoke, albeit we were happy with silence or the low volume of a local radio station in the background.

(Yulia with her parents showing me around Yasnaya Polyana.)

I got settled into the flat and, moments later, Yulia came in and caught my eye, which I was not ready for. She was wearing a lady's black suit; she looked attractive, professional, and she was radiant. I kept that thought away and to enjoy time together which was great, as Yulia could speak more English. It was not perfect, but it was much better than my Russian, that's for sure. The translation books came out every so often to help, but we were able to converse more freely than we did before. It was a relaxing holiday which I so needed, and it was lovely to see Tula in the sunshine and places of Yasnaya Polyana. Within a few days of being there with Yulia, I started to take a bit of a shine to her and felt that she was a lovely lady with such a fantastic nature, but, although I still didn't want her to know, I did drop a few hints. One hint was where I got changed in my room before night-time and Yulia asked if I had changed so that she could enter the room with a cup of tea. I told her to enter but I was without a shirt. Not that I thought it was naughty in anyway, as men are often shirtless on the beach or walking on the street when it's sunny. Plus, I felt ugly with my body shape, especially with being overweight. Yulia was still a bit embarrassed as to think where to put her eyes during our conversation, so maybe she was thinking I was a bit attractive. At least that's what I thought.

There was one problem getting worse during the holiday for me whilst staying in the flat, which was that I had a cat allergy and Yulia had two of them. My breathing got worse with a death rattle type sound coming from my throat or chest, and therefore I had to open the windows to get air in at night. This opening attracted mosquitoes to enter the room, so I became like a dartboard to where they aimed at my body. So not only was I overweight, with bite marks all over my body, but to top it off, I had difficulties breathing. I was feeling less attractive day by day. I was feeling less healthy day by day too.

The holiday was drawing to an end and Anya, Yulia's daughter, was conversing in Russian, of course, but I heard her say "Papa" a few times. I asked Yulia what she was speaking about, and Yulia said, in an embarrassed manner, that Anya liked me as her Daddy. That was very flattering to me but I was not sure how Yulia felt, plus, it was still a big task to be in a relationship with someone living in another country and with being a Step-Dad. The penultimate day before my flight back changed everything as we visited Moscow. I saw the same things as before, the Kremlin and Red Square, but this time we went to look at the Great Church of Moscow. Sitting outside on the park bench near this huge building, Anya started get a little jealous of me having attention so her Mum gave her an idea to find the biggest fallen leaf on the ground, which was discovered after a ten minute search. Anya was a happy bunny when she got the attention of comparing the smaller leaves against the amazing maple leaf. I sat there looking at how Yulia was with her daughter and looking at this awesome white building with golden globes on top, and it was a very surreal time. I was not all that keen on history in that time of my life, but I was still very impressed by the interior artwork and how beautiful it all was. The amazing element was that I was in Moscow and in the heart of this wonderful building. Yulia and I sat on one of the benches inside, looking up at the religious artwork, and conversation began naturally about life and experiences. The conversation grew deeper, and I mentioned the time of when I nearly died as a baby and later of the near-death experience as a teenager. Tears flew from Yulia's eyes at that moment. It was pure connection, and warm feelings came through our minds. I immediately naturally embraced Yulia to say that everything is fine now and I was ok, that those times had gone but changed me. Whilst holding her in my arms, I did not want the moment to end, and it was discovered in later conversation that neither did Yulia. I was concerned of Yulia's Dad showing up at any time, as he was busy taking photos at that moment with his wife. If Yulia's Dad saw us arm-in-arm with each other I would most certainly get told off, or so I thought at the time. The embrace was delicate and tentative. It was from that moment that all of our lives would change forever. The journey on the way to their flat in Tula was quiet, as Yulia had told her parents earlier about what just happened. It was not frowned upon by her parents at all, as they knew she could make her own choices in life, but it was the emotion which exhausted us both. Combined with a long day of travelling to Moscow and sight-seeing, we decided to rest our eyes. It gave us time to reflect on that moment, and think about the 'what ifs' in our lives. The next day arrived, and it was the day of the flight. It was time for me to put my heart on my sleeve, and I said that I was going to miss Yulia and Anya. From that instance in the kitchen, we embraced, long and tight together. Looking into each other's eyes, we almost kissed, but we went back to embracing. It was too soon to kiss each other and we both felt it would be wrong to be more intimate just before I was about to fly away. It had to be at the right time.

At the airport I sat on the suitcases, as there were very little seating areas outside. It was when Yulia's Dad went to park up the car that I invited Yulia to sit on the case with me, and she squashed up next to me. I trembled when I put my arm around her waist, but those nerves were quashed when her hand went on mine. Our fingers rubbed and played with each other, which set off fireworks in my head. The farewell was a sad one and I fought back the tears, but it was obvious that it was the same for Yulia. Yulia returned home to discover a note in her room which I had written that morning. This note stated what a brilliant Mum she was and that she had a lovely daughter. Yulia could not carry on with her boyfriend from that day onwards. She told her boyfriend that it was over. The newly ex-boyfriend thought that Yulia was crazy to finish it all over a holiday romance. She replied that it was more than that and, in fact, Yulia and I did not even kiss. To tell the truth, I was hoping to visit again soon and I was really interested in her. I landed in London where the wheelchair help that I asked for was very late and, after a long wait, I told the staff that I would go by myself on my crutches. With my hand luggage on my back, off I went, as I was concerned for my parents waiting to collect me on the other side. It was a long way to get to my main luggage and with difficulties in breathing because of the cat allergy, which escalated to being a lot worse during that stay. Once my luggage was collected, I then walked without my crutches as I could not carry luggage with them. It was getting too much to take, and I almost collapsed from exhaustion. I thought I was on the verge of having a heart attack, as I felt my heart pounding against my ribs. Sweat was seeping through the light brown coat I was wearing but carrying the coat would only make it worse. By that point, my Dad spotted me in such difficulties and he went over the lines to collect his son when a guard stopped him. My Dad replied, "Look at my son struggling over there", so the chap and my Dad came to my rescue. Once seated in the car, I drank two bottles of orange juice and got rehydrated again. When I had got my breath back and felt ready to talk, I told my parents about my feelings for Yulia. I broke down in tears thinking that I had just left behind a lady that I truly loved, and who loved me too. My parents encouraged me to continue to write and, above all, talk to Yulia on the phone.

I rang Yulia as soon as I got home and, from then on, I rang her every day. We emailed each other still as it was nice to write more about feelings and, for me, it was easier to write than to say things. Over time, our correspondence got more detailed and so did the phone calls sometimes, where the calls would be an hour or longer. It was important to us both to make this regular contact, and Skype came in handy; to have a connection by seeing each other's reactions by webcam was superb.

It was during this period that my Mum took over my diet. My Mum made me good healthy foods with vegetables and fruit desserts, as chocolate was off the menu. I visited my parents in the week and brought back lots of frozen ready-made meals from my Mum. Within a year, I had lost about two stone in weight and was feeling really well for it. Plus, my drinking habit decreased somewhat but I still drank, as I secretly thought that this possible relationship was never going to happen. I thought that, one day, she would take off her rose-tinted spectacles, see this ogre in all his glory, and cancel the whole thing. I just had no self-value as the schooling period in my life with all the bullying had taken it away from me. I believed, and the conversations inside my head believed, that I was not worthy of being on planet Earth. I felt I was never going to fit into the normality of things, so I saw my parents or called them and then later rang Yulia. A little bit later after talking, I would hit the bottle as I just had this self-destruct button.

Soon, Yulia came over to England in the springtime and it was a nervous time for us both. The question on our minds was; would we feel the same as when I was in Russia? This question was overturned when we met at the airport and hugged each other. From there, we drove down to Torquay with Lee and Kate in the back seat, as Kate flew with Yulia to England. The journey down to Torquay was a few hours so, with Lee and Kate sleeping, I managed to touch Yulia's hand and she responded with the same. On arrival in Torquay, we were shown to our room and that's where we stayed. We stayed for hours, which became days. Shouts from behind the door would be heard occasionally, such as, 'Ok you lovebirds, that's enough' or 'Yulia, do you not want to see England on your visit, or just say you visited the bed?' The voices behind the door obviously came from Lee or Kate getting frustrated by not seeing their friends. So, with a bit of the encouragement from Lee and Kate, Yulia did see some places of Torquay. Later, we travelled up to Derby for the rest of the week where Yulia met my parents, later my friends and, of course, my Nana. The holiday cemented our romance and we knew now that we wanted to be together. I travelled a few more times to Russia to bond with Yulia's parents and friends and with little Anya, who was happy to call me her Dad, or Papa. I was getting very proud of calling Anya my daughter. Yulia travelled again to England a few more times too, and experienced new places and food which I wanted to impress upon Yulia. I also visited Russia a few more times. One memory that I could not shake out from my mind was an actual streaker! We were waiting in the departure lounge at the airport with Kate, Lee's wife, as she was visiting at the same time. It was all quiet and subdued when all of a sudden, loud shouting came from somewhere behind us. It was a man's voice shouting in Russian. He emerged shirtless at that moment and then trouserless (new word for the dictionary?), and off came the pants. Following this, the security guys came running after him. He and his bare arse scarpered down the terminal and towards the plane. I think he really wanted to fly urgently and take a bath. All we could hear was the man screaming when the security caught up with him but we never saw him again, strange that?

As time went by in our relationship, talks began emerging between Yulia and I about marriage and where to live together. It was questioned about Russia; could I live in Russia, could I learn the language, could I get a job there, could the environment and people be ok with me being disabled? Then the other side of the coin was the question of could Yulia and Anya live in England with matters of work and schooling, and so on. It was eventually discovered that there would be more pros than cons if Yulia and Anya came to live in England. We set a date to be married in Russia on the 28th February 2008, which just so happened to be a day earlier than my parents who married on 1st March, obviously discounting leap years.

Chapter 17

Gor'kiy

Unfortunately, my dad had been struggling with arthritis in this period of my life and he had to have a knee replacement a few months before the wedding was to take place. There was no chance that he would be able to fly and my Mum was still looking after him, so without my parents on the big day meant that I wanted to enjoy the time with Yulia, Anya, and my family-in-law-to-be. Later on, maybe I would organise a ceremony in England. Basically, I felt that if my parents were not attending the Russian wedding, it was both pointless and too expensive in asking anyone else to be there. One funny occasion happened to be that, on the journey over to be married, I travelled on the same plane as Top Gear presenter, amongst many other shows, James May. I had to do a double take to make sure it was him but when I saw how he smiled and then I heard his voice, yes, that was James May alright. He made his way to his seat with a few other people and it just so happened that he was only a few rows back from me, perfect. Once the pilot turned off the 'no seatbelt' sign, I was compelled to shake James's hand and say how brilliant he was. James looked narked somewhat, and tired of how many times it happened already, so I thought not to outstay my welcome and returned to my seat. I felt a bit embarrassed that James was not happy, as I did not see anyone else going over and now I had made it obvious that there was a celebrity on the plane.

The big day came for Yulia and I to be married, but my concerns still rearing their ugly heads; maybe she will get cold feet because she cannot stand the look of me, especially when marriage is so final. Yulia and I, as tradition goes, slept in different flats. I sent a text to her to wish her 'good night, sleep well, and see you in the morning', and her reply calmed my mind when she responded with the same. I could not believe I was actually getting married the next day and in Russia, of all places, so the first clairvoyant that I met when I was twenty years of age was correct all along. I had forgotten by the time I was thirty five all that he said, as I thought it not possible. This wedding was going to be different for one reason; Yulia had been married before, and so she chose to have a turquoise dress rather than white. When I saw her approach towards the registry office, she was stunning, beautiful, and radiant. However, the wedding was not going to be all the fun and games of Lee and Kate's wedding earlier, as it was going to be difficult to carry Yulia over a bridge for starters.

The ceremony was held at a wedding registry office where Yulia worked as a violinist in a quartet. The lady who held the ceremony knew Yulia very well, and she gave a wonderful and emotional service. It was emotional for all including, of course, Yulia and I, with Anya right next to us holding onto a posy of flowers. I had a translator throughout as to understand it all, enabling me to kiss my new wife when I was prompted. Yulia and I had to make it official with signing in the registry book of marriages which had Russian language, so I had no clue what I was signing for but, joking aside, I knew it was legitimate. It was all done and dusted; we were officially married. Then, Yulia and I had a stampede of guests coming over to shake our hands or close relatives to give us. All the guests present wished us a long and happy marriage. It helped so much to have my translator next to me, as I would not have a clue what was being wished, but I was amazed that some spoke very good English.

(Yulia, Anya and I after registering our wedding.)

After the celebratory drinks and cake in the registry office, it was time for all to go back home to rest a bit as there was the party in the evening. The wedding evening was held at a restaurant where Yulia also played violin to entertain the diners. When Yulia got out of the taxi, a few games were prepared before we could enter the venue. One of these was a simple gesture of letting go of our previous life of being single by releasing two balloons to symbolise it.

There was alcohol galore on all tables; bottles of wine, champagne, vodka, oh, and bottles of water for those who wanted to take a break from drinking. Right behind our table was a huge heart made from red balloons, and the whole venue was decorated so beautifully. Again, there were games where I had to show how strong I was and how fast Yulia was. Then, my in-laws were brought up by the host of the evening where they had to show how to kiss correctly, so that Yulia and I can have a long and happy marriage like they have. They kissed for what seemed like ages, and then it was time for us to have a go. Yulia and I also kissed for what seemed like forever but it was deemed as disappointing to all those watching, as they encouraged us to kiss for longer, to which we did until it was approved with shouts of hooray. There was plenty of kissing from Yulia and I that night, as people celebrating would shout out 'gor'kiy' which, when translated, means 'bitter'. The champagne they tasted was bitter until we, the newly married couple, kissed to make it taste sweet. 'Gor'kiy' was shouted out every five minutes by someone or other. My parents then came on the television, fed to us by satellite, and they did a speech for us which was recorded by a camcorder. It was emotional to hear the kind words they had to say. The same went for the kind words from Yulia's family and close friends. There was lots of food for all to enjoy, even red caviar so I thought to give it a go. Bad idea! It was just like crunching rock salt in my mouth. It was rumoured amongst the rich folks that it was yummy, but it was quite the opposite, more like! After the food was finished, it was time to dance. It was the first song of the evening where the newly-wedded couple traditionally had to dance first and, as you are aware by now, that happens in Russia too, but for me to dance... It was not going to happen. So, Yulia's Dad took the lead, dancing with his daughter to Abba's song of 'I do, I do, I do', which was apt for a wedding night. He picked her up in his strong arms in one surprising swoop for Yulia, where her surprised face was a picture indeed. She was shocked by her Dad's strength, and then she was swayed by the beat of the music in her Dad's arms. Her Dad, still dancing with her in his arms, brought her to me, where we danced (or swayed!) whilst sitting on the chairs together. Everyone else then got up to dance in true Russian style!

Yulia loved to dance, and that's what she did onwards. I

watched her as she drifted off into her own world, which is where dancing took her. Yulia's eyes and expression are just wonderful to see; it looks like pure bliss when she's dancing to the rhythm. I just wished I could be up there with her and feel that emotion too, but I had no choice. I had people coming over to wish me well from left, right, and centre. People who knew me had already toasted with me, like Yulia's best friend, Nadya. Then, Yulia's other best friends of Alex and Sverta congratulated me with a toast then drink or few, or multiplied by four. Then, my new Father-in-Law came for a toast and drink, but multiply that by five. At the end of the evening, I was completely drunk, plus I had extremely red eyes from both the cocktails of alcohol and the allergy to rubber, as the heart-shaped balloons behind me had managed to reach me just from being near; rubber was my Kryptonite! Before you jump to making condom jokes, I have already heard them. Jokes like, 'Doctor, can you stop this allergy from being so painful but keep the swelling'. If you Google 'Spina Bifida and latex allergy', you will come across a strange connection; a lot of Spina Bifida folks have the allergy, funny that! Although it's not a funny allergy and I count myself lucky that I just get swollen and sore eyes. I heard that latex allergies can be fatal so, yes, I am lucky!

Anyhow, back to the wedding night. I was worse for wear. I managed to get to the taxi and into the flat but, after that, I was out completely. I had torn off my shirt and could not remember anything else until I woke up the next day, much to Yulia's dismay. Once the hangover had dwindled throughout the day, we packed up and set off to a hotel in Yasnaya Pollyana. It was a lovely place; the room where we stayed was romantic and the ideal place to celebrate this momentous time together.

Anya was looked after by her grandparents as they did so often, like when Yulia was on holiday in England, working in the evenings, or studying in the daytime. On the first morning in the hotel, we were woken up by my mobile phone ringing; a man on the other end of the phone stated he was from Radio Derby and wanted to know what it was like being in Russia and married. I was totally confused as to how he knew all of this, and where the conversation was going. The radio presenter advised that it was not just a random call and he said that one person had set it all up. I interrupted him politely, as I knew already who it may be. "Let me guess, was it my Dad, by any chance?" Indeed, it was; my Dad came on the phone laughing and the conversation was aired live on Radio Derby. Luckily, no-one swore at the time. It felt like my parents were in Russia with me on this call and it felt like they really wanted to be there to share their son's experience. Once the phone call ended, I looked at my beautiful wife and said, 'my Dad'. It was enough to know he was up to no good, which I guess I had gotten my mischievous nature from. It was great for both Yulia and I to call each other husband and wife as it was new to us both; it was strange, but it gave us nice feelings. It was strange to see the gold bands on our fingers. It was noticed that one wedding present of two crystal glasses were broken. It was a bad Russian omen for the wedding if one was broken, but if a second was broken then it cancelled it out. Luckily, I broke the second one by 'accident', which relieved Yulia's feelings. Time was approaching fast for me to leave Russia again, though, and to be back at work. The gruelling plans now lay ahead, and that was to bring my wife and daughter over to stay in England.

It was documents galore to send to embassies with passports, birth certificates, and application forms to fill out to get the ball rolling. It was also a big possibility that the powers that be could decide not to approve the application, and that would then mean to challenge that decision. It would cost extra money to dispute their findings as to why they disallowed the Visas to live in the United Kingdom. Whilst that was all being processed, I had questions in my mind; the one bedroom property, the little 'Norther's Nest' would not be adequate for when Yulia and Anya arrived. If they arrived, was the other question. However, I could not dwell on the 'what ifs' and had to make tracks on where to live next. I also really wanted to leave this home, as I still felt that the vision at the time of my NDE could come true. I looked around many properties and liked a lot of them where I could see nice bedrooms for Anya to enjoy and gardens to run around in. I put my home on the market and one person was interested, but that man was not able to sell his own house. The buying and selling of each other's home would begin the normal process but then we would hear that the person selling their home had people pulled out, which happened twice, so the circle was never completed. The great news came that it was fine for Yulia and Anya to live in the UK, but this meant that I had to be faster at getting that bigger place to live together. With the great news of Yulia and Anya being able to live in the UK, I then bought flight tickets in August. It had to happen before September, as Anya had to be enrolled into school. I thought to maybe buy the property of the man who wanted 'Northers' Nest'. The mortgage was going to be slightly more than what I wished for but my hands were beginning to be tied by time. I looked around the chap's home and I loved it. It had a huge garden for my daughter to run around in, three bedrooms, and the place had a homely feel to it. The agreement to swap homes was under way. Believe it or not, but my house swap literally happened just one week prior to my family from Russia arriving. It was so close that it could have been the other way around.

I drove down to Heathrow to pick up my new family with excitement in my stomach. I sat waiting at the arrivals and it seemed that everyone was going through, but where were Yulia and Anya? They had gotten stuck in the passport control section, as Yulia needed to prove she was Anya's Mum because of the difference in surnames. Once out of arrivals and hugs given all around, the drive home was next. It was Anya's first time in England, of course, and she was excited about it all. Both Yulia and Anya were understandably tired from the flight over. Yulia was tired from the emotion of saying her farewells to her nearest and dearest. I decided that we needed to take a halfway break at a petrol station and café bar. It was a realisation in my mind that this is it, we did it! It was now reality that we are a family, and what was the future to hold? The nearest future was that I, along with my parents, planned a wedding blessing/party. This was not really organised on a whim as invites had to be sent out but it was a risk if they, Yulia and Anya, would be there or not. The party evening went well as relatives, friends, and colleagues from work were there. There were people there that I knew well, like Betty who helped me so much in the Secondary School. Yulia had invited her violin teacher, who was living in Germany, to travel over for the occasion. Thankfully, I also asked a chap, Michael, who worked in the same organisation who was also a priest. Now, as you may know by now, I was not heavily religious but, to have our wedding blessed by such a wonderful friend, it had to be done. Not only was Michael a priest but he was also a keen photographer and an all-round music addict that would blow my socks off with how much music he knew more than me. Michael did such a great job as he blessed us, and it felt so warm and loving. Yulia was a little shy in talking English with the crowd watching us, but we stated our vows to love each other for better and for worse, which was emotional for all concerned. Then it came to Ashley's (who flew from Madeira) revenge as I invited him to be the best man for the blessing and now it was time for his speech. Ashley gave the history of the family from many generations where all the couples met, fell in love, and married, all of which came from Derby. Then Ashley mentioned about him marrying a German lady and then me marrying a Russian lady, and how it had basically put an end to the Northridge tradition. Ashley told the audience about the time when I was up to the waist in plaster, when we accidentally broke the plaster, and that story made so many people chuckle. This time I was not drunk, compared to the wedding night in Russia, as I was driving, therefore I was also able to remember the night and to be coherent to talk to everyone there!

It was all well and good having holidays backwards and forwards during our courtship, but it was nothing like living together forever. Yulia and I did experiment somewhat during the holiday periods that either I or Yulia worked so that it was nearly like normal life and not just a holiday. However, now we were a family and there were difficulties, at first, to settle in. Of course, both Yulia and Anya were missing their previous lifestyles. For example, Yulia had not been working for almost a year since her arrival. The way of life in Russia for Yulia was a busy one. As you know by now, she was a musician, and a talented one at that. She played in orchestras, quartets, and as a soloist, but then she studied in Business Management. Now, living in Derby, she only had four walls to look at constantly whilst I was at work, and it was getting claustrophobic. All she would know about was the movements of her next door neighbours which weren't appealing, so we were trying so hard to get her into work. Yulia started by helping as a childminding assistant. It was not really adequate money, but it got Yulia's mind focused on her work, by planning and helping children with fun activities. She eventually played at a local orchestra which was good for her to get her violin out again, practice at home, and then rehearse with the orchestra to achieve their goal of playing at a local venue. It lasted just about a year for Yulia but there were fees to pay for each member of the orchestra to play, so it was not financially attractive to keep going. Briefly, let me take you back to the wedding blessing as I, wanting to impress Yulia plus possibly give her links with fellow musicians, hired a string quartet. I had kept the quartet's email and wrote to them for advice of what, where, and how to help Yulia build her music career. She was then asked to play with the quartet which was not brilliant for Yulia, as it was on the spot reading music sheets, whereas Yulia preferred to rehearse together so, again, that fizzled out. However, Yulia kept in contact with the viola player, Sarah. Later, Sarah and Yulia performed at venues together with an established accompanist couple, Neil and Jane on the piano. Since meeting that couple, Yulia hosted other concerts in the Derbyshire region. Yulia performed in concerts for charity, where she raised so much money to help Spina Bifida children. Yulia also raised money for a local church and for a local school.

Chapter 18

Settling In

Let me tell you about Anya; she did not know much English at all when she arrived to England. She had a few lessons in Russia before she came to stay but it was the very basics. To converse with each other, Anya and I had to have Yulia translating, and then there would be times where the conversation between mother and daughter would go off. I could not understand any of it and only found out later what the conversation was about. Anya, who had only been in England since August 2008, would be thrown into the deep end and be sent to school the following month with only a few English words in her vocabulary. The school was amazing for her, as the teachers were both helpful and patient. Anya made a friend at school on the first day, Simone, who helped her so very much in her language and confidence. Before Yulia and I knew it, Anya was speaking very well indeed in both languages. She hadn't a Russian accent either and, in fact, it was more of a Derbyshire dialect where she would miss out her letter 't' in words, saying things like "wa'er" or "will you gerit Dad, please?" She had taken up the violin as a hobby, also, under Mum's supervision and training. She took up a few other interests too, as most children do until they decide what they want. She eventually landed into a place called Centre Stage where she learnt singing, dancing, and acting. She performed at a few shows, like a pantomime, Cowboys and Aliens, and Joseph and the Amazing Technicolour Dreamcoat. She even played a higher position of the last concert of Cosette in Les Misérables, which I was extremely proud to watch. Yulia did not get the chance to see as she was the violinist for the ensemble of Les Mis. It was the first time seeing this musical and, to be honest, I was in tears throughout as the storyline was incredibly emotional.

I was pants at helping Anya with any homework as I struggled to remember the stuff I learnt at school. I remember all the good and bad things, but the education bit had gone for a Burton. So, when Anya asked anything Mathematical when homework was too tough, she would say, "Dad..." then, after thinking again, she would shout, "Mum..." as she got to know that Dad's limits are just the five times tables. However, when it comes to spelling, I am the Daddy. I don't know why, but spelling is ok for me; ask me about nouns or pronouns and I would not have a clue. I just write and talk but would not say, "Oh, that was a pronoun that I just said".

The greatest and best thing that warmed my heart is that Anya chose me to be her Dad even before Yulia and I became a couple. There is no 'Step-Dad' mentioned in any conversation, as I am Dad to her. The next thing is that I want to adopt Anya so that it is all legally binding.

Whilst Yulia was taking Anya to school one day with a violin strapped to her back, Yulia and the head teacher struck up a conversation; the head teacher never knew that Yulia played. They arranged to meet in the head's office and talk about possibly working for free but to help children to learn more about music. It was arranged that Yulia did an after-school club, and that took off so well that it went on after the term-time. This then snowballed for Yulia to have a job via the local council. She went on to build up her classes from there and, like teaching is, she has good and bad days. There is a lot of preparation involved, and most of the time she would get to bed at 3am as the hardest part is translation and to understand documents. I try to help as much as possible with spelling checks and grammar when I come home from work, although I admit it is not always possible in the job that I have. The last thing I want to do when I am home is sometimes to talk; it must be a man thing. I once read 'Men are from Mars, Women Are from Venus' and it was true that men need to go into their cave at times. Yulia is very good at knowing this and gives me time out, and a mutual respect of our feelings keeps the marriage stronger.

We have settled in very nicely without a doubt. It was hard for me in some ways though as I was single for most of my life, and adapting to not being single was a bit hard. I could not come and go as I did as a single man, although I was not the type to go out at night clubbing, but it was the feeling of restriction. It was also my stubbornness or my independence which always got me into trouble. It derived from the times in my childhood when I would dream of being self-sufficient, so when things happen like I could not get my socks on due to pains in my legs or arthritis making it more of a challenge, I would then start getting grumpy by loudly muttering and tuttering, being careful not to swear when my daughter was around! Things like drying my feet after a wash was a chore that I found hard to reach. My tactic to dry my legs was to use a towel like a whip; if you were behind the bathroom door, you'd hear me grunt and a whack, and you'd wonder what on earth I was doing in there. I find it is difficult to be able to walk around the house well as age has started to wear at my legs. Yulia had to learn to have the patience of Job. Yet she helps me now to dry my feet all the time, as it is important to regularly check for sores or cuts. I became a dab hand at cooking; it was by watching cooking shows on television that inspired me, plus I wished I kept cooking lessons going at school. I would not have been able to become a chef as it looks like more of an able-bodied job and extremely stressful with all the shouting at each other. The kitchen in our home, sadly, was on the small side, which made it difficult to cook as a couple, so with long conversations with each other, the plan was set to build an extension to the kitchen. It took a lot of financial planning and to find the right people for the job but, from there, things escalated. The building itself got erected so fast that Yulia and I thought it would be done within months, but we were wrong. It took time to get the steel work calculations done and then the mistake that we made was to wait to find the right kitchen, as the ordering took a very long time to arrive. Eating a lot of microwave meals, takeaways, and sandwiches, then washing dishes in the bath every night was getting to be unpleasant, so paper plates and cups helped instead. Finally, the kitchen was in, apart from the fridge freezer. We asked the fitter why he did not fit it and he said it would not fit as the design was incorrectly done! So, with that, we measured the gap and the fridge freezer and thought, with millimetres to spare, it would go in. Off we went to move it from the living room where the fridge freezer had sat for six weeks. There was a lot of "to me, to you"' as Yulia and I rocked the appliance over to the slot. The appliance fitted in perfectly and we gave each other a high five only to then open the door and find that the door was catching the wall on the hinge, so it opened by five inches, which was useless. We simply had to swap the appliance for a type that we really did not like too much, but we had no other option.

It was then that the cooker was tried for the first time. Boy, we were ready for proper homemade food! I hasten to add that I was the kind of guy that would do first then, if all fails, to read the instructions. The induction hob was turned on and I prepared all the food ready for a Spaghetti Bolognese. The pans went on to the hob and the ingredients went in next, when I realised that there's nothing happening. I checked the temperature and, after five minutes, the food in the pans was cold. Okay, I thought, now for the instructions to come out, and it basically read that an induction hob requires induction type pans, so off to the supermarket I went! Since the kitchen went in, we have already enjoyed so many lovely meals and a lot of time spent together in the extended room. The builders also altered the downstairs cloakroom into a toilet room, and that had been a godsend as I no longer had to trawl up the stairs when desperate for the loo.

In this time in my life, I am at the most happiest I have ever been. I have a great wife, daughter, and family behind me. Things are changing so much with age, as it does to all. I am getting a lot of grey and white hairs coming through, which are more noticeable when I haven't shaved! Arthritis is more poignant, which means that there is more of the pain factor to put up with. I have more restricted mobility, and thus had to invest in a wheelchair for longer distances. With help of the wheelchair, I have enjoyed time with my family around zoos and amusement parks. Although, saying that, there was a moment where I escaped death once again, as one park had a very steep hill and, whilst going downhill, Yulia could no longer grip the handle bars with my weight of eighteen stone and I was struggling to hold onto the wheels. As the wall approached, I could see the horizon behind and, basically, it was going to be a sheer drop afterwards. So, I ignored the pains in my hands whilst gripping the wheels and putting out my left foot, managing to just stop a few feet away from the wall. However, I did have visions of flying through the air with the momentum of hitting the wall like something from a Tom and Jerry cartoon.

Chapter 19

Black Stuff

I continued to work full-time at a housing association, booking in repairs of customers' homes, although it's a very stressful and energy-sapping job, so I take each day as it comes. It is quite a grumpy environment to work in, to say the least. First of all, the customers expect customer service where it is still acceptable to shout at the member of staff just so that they can get their own way. Shouting at the employee does not mean that they will get their own way, but it gets it off their chest, I guess. Secondly, people are forever using their circumstances to get their own way, where they would freely say that they have a disability just so that they can beat the date of repair by one day. Or, they would use their children as though it was a disability with the often question asked, "Do you expect me to manage without a boiler for two days? I have five children, how shall I cope?" The thought crops up of, well, you decided to have that number of children, and you decided to be on benefits rather than getting a job. It just feels like a victim culture that we are now living in. The funny conversation arrives when the television aerial is not working and the priority of having that repaired is within a week. All hell is let loose down the phone with how people cannot cope once their TV programmes are taken away from them. The tenants would ask how they can entertain their children now that the box in the corner is no longer working. It is a tongue-biting moment when I struggle from withholding sentences similar to this, "Play board games, talk to each other (heaven forbid!), write, read a book and, if the worst comes to the worst, get a DVD!" I must say that I am not heavily political, but when it affects how I am at home after being shouted at on a lot of calls, it equals a grumpy husband and Dad being at home. People just want everything for nothing and Britain is breeding this culture. It doesn't make people get up off their bottoms to work and be proud. It was my Dad's encouragement to be that fighter and not to sit on my bottom. I did not think it was the way to be, moping about my disability; Dad encouraged me to be positive and to keep on my feet. Even when I was on the verge of suicide and depression, I continued to work, as it kept my momentum going. To have a focus in life and not to blame others is the way forward.

Recently, I had a fair few falls and a car accident which has caused problems with my lower back. The pain increased, and I asked a GP to have another painkiller, which was prescribed, and the pain subsided. However, nearly a week later, I felt unwell most of Saturday, and was thinking the fast food may have caused it. I had bought a burger as I was so hungry and did not get the chance to cook at that time, but these instances were rare. To counteract the horrid indigestion, I was drinking milk and taking remedies for heartburn. This was not improving in any way and, in fact, the ripping pain in my chest was increasing. It got to the point where, at night, I was no longer able to sleep but did not want to disturb my wife anymore as she had already got up twice to bring milk and tablets, so off I went downstairs. During the pain I was thinking to myself that it was a possible heart-attack as the pain felt like around an eight or nine on a scale of one to ten. I was being sick with black stuff, and the same black stuff came from diarrhoea, which was concerning. I went on to the internet to discover that I needed to ring 111, which was the number to use instead of 999 as it was urgent, but not an emergency. They diagnosed that it was not a heart attack, and that it was a possible internal bleeding. Within ten minutes, the paramedics came with heart monitoring equipment and confirmed that it was not a heart attack but that there were irregular heartbeats when the pain entered my chest. Later, the ambulance arrived to take me to hospital where I had a doctor check on me. After the blood pressure and temperature check, I asked if it was okay to check my bottom as blood had come out from there. I gave permission but did not know a finger would go up next, which was definitely unexpected and a first life experiences. The A&E area was so busy that it took time to have the results of the blood tests, and so on. However, during this wait with Yulia at my side, I was noticing the pain coming in more often and, eventually, it was every five minutes. The painkilling medicine just came back up when I was sick, so then morphine was given intravenously. To cut longer story short, the medicines that I had taken for my bad back had caused ulcers to form and burst near my chest area. I was without food for a good few days and lost half a stone in weight, which was a positive note for me. During my stay in hospital, it gave me time to reflect on this episode so much. Yulia was most upset about the reality that if it was something more severe, like a heart attack and that I had let her sleep, I could have collapsed downstairs without anyone knowing. Mr Independent now feels that I should be thinking less of others and to be more aware that next time, heaven forbid that it does happen again, I would make sure that Yulia was awake and informed.

Chapter 20

Presentless

Ok, so you know the ins and outs about me but let me give you more of an insight to my life, and the positives and negatives of being disabled.

Things not to do:

Go to the Great Wall of China, avoid a trip to see the Major Oak, pee whilst standing up as balance is terrible and it's difficult to avoid spraying the guy standing next to you.

I can get leg room on the plane and assistance in the airport, sometimes! Plus, you can get to sit on one of those train thingybobs (another word in the dictionary, please?) that whizz from one terminal to the next. Being disabled, you can go around the larger supermarkets in a rented scooter that they have with a basket, thus ending the stress of using crutches with a basket, which is a difficult task. Just to walk from the car, get one item (when not really paying attention to detail in the rush and getting wrong item), then pay for it, and get back to the car can make you completely cream-crackered; apologies for the cockney rhyming slang.

I get my shoes for free, although they are nothing like anything anyone has ever seen before, so they draw attention. I can only have a few pairs a year and therefore have to repair regularly, meaning they look scuffed somewhat, usually. I have the chance to go on a lot of rides, like the London Eye, where my wife is deemed as my carer and gets a cheaper rate of tickets. I can get help from the government for benefits, and its ok in my mind that I can have this extra help to have a nice car through Motability. Yes, there are some people who take advantage and fake a bad back or something alike which sparks debates, but it is great for the ones who truly need it.

The minor things in life, for example finding lost keys around the house, spends more energy than you may think, and then I am knackered for the rest of the day. Plus, the outcome is a more-than-usual messy house and I cannot tidy with the previously mentioned knackeredness (I am determined to get a least one new word in the dictionary!). When you have a disability, planning is everything in life, for example, if there are no nearby parking spaces when going to a shop, then have a plan B and either circle around until a space becomes free or have a second shop nearby to park at. In order to go from one room to the next, you have to plan how to carry things or put things on the floor while crawling and moving the objects slowly and surely between the rooms. The same goes for going upstairs with things. When you have to go out and accidentally meet people you know, if a conversation drums up, you have to make a random excuse to break it, otherwise it would mean a crawl back to the car and not being able to carry out the reason for going out in the first place.

When going to parties, especially ones with buffets where people are queuing at the tables, you have a choice. The first option is to ask either a friend or a relative to get food for you whilst they get it for themselves. This results in the other person looking like he or she is greedy by taking two plates, and it's also a risk of getting things like egg mayonnaise sandwiches, which is purely evil (maybe that's too strong of a term, horrid is probably better). The second option is to have someone, again, queue for you, and then you join them when they get near the front, which looks like you have queue-jumped, and that is not the English way! The third and final option is to take a plate and, while using your crutches, take what you want and risk the food falling all over the floor as you're taking it to the table. This means, really, that you should actually eat until you're totally full prior to the party in order to avoid these issues, or see all of the other people stuff their faces and then go home and eat until sick. Don't drink alcohol at the parties, and driving makes a good excuse to stay sober. However, if you have a disability and you need a toilet, it is pot luck with what you get; whether it be a broken toilet seat or dirty toilet, then it is bad luck. The reason why you shouldn't drink, though, let's face it, it's a challenge to walk in the first place, let alone if you're drunk! Then, there's the usual dancing at the party with 'Agadoo' or 'The Birdie Song' which looks like fun, but you would look like a complete muppet as walking is difficult already, let alone dancing. However, if you're single and dancing, you have permission to hold a lady without being arrested. This is painful to watch (from a disabled viewpoint), as you only wished that you could do the same, so make your excuses and leave early. Driving is difficult, but a requirement if you can when you're disabled. It means that the right car is so important; for me, it had to have room for my right foot to have space to put it to one side. Otherwise, it would mean that the foot would touch the accelerator without knowing because of paralysis, which would not be a good result. It would be more complicated if there was more adaptation, but I was fortunate to have only an automatic car. Carrying heavy loads, mowing the lawns, going up ladders to clean windows, cleaning the car, vacuum cleaning and so on, are things that I can never do, which I guess many of you readers would be grateful for. Although this means that I have to ask for another person to do them, which is frustrating and that means of course a very busy, multi-tasking wife! It also brings in another viewpoint which I would like to have your attention for, and that is political correctness. Now, years ago when I was more sensitive about being disabled, I was adamant that I was independent to the point where I was rude, like I felt I was to my Secondary School carer. The point where I am now means that I need help so much more and

I must bite my tongue while gracefully accepting help. But the public, here in the UK, are completely confused as to what to do when they see someone disabled struggling to go through a door or something. Some disabled people can get fiery when someone offers help, as I have seen it too. To the other extreme, I have seen disabled folks struggle and it's ignored by public. It's just that there is confusion as to what to do at these times. It kind of gives me a thought, should those who are independent choose to wear a certain badge, the same as our blue badge holders showing that we are allowed to park in those disabled spaces? Maybe a certain badge can be worn to show, "Hey, I am an easy-going person who will help you and, in turn, you can help me?" That would be cool in my mind, and maybe that may happen. Political correctness is that folks are correcting themselves, or others, as to what can be said or not said. It's like what George Carlin, an amazing comedian, once said, and I'll paraphrase. The words are not the insulting issue here, it is the person who is saying those words, as the words are innocent. There's too many ism's; sexism, racism, and so on. These ism's, in my mind, were created by 'them'; the powers who hide behind the curtain like in the Wizard of Oz, and then the folks take it as their own to make it a part of their identity. But, if they did not know these isms existed, then maybe they would not take it on board. I personally say that no matter what gender, race, ability, your body is just the vehicle which your soul travels in during that lifetime, and there is no need to have any disagreements with others. We, as humans who share this blue and green dot in the universe, must see the bigger picture. These isms are there to divide us and 'they' are conquering, making us busy fighting/arguing on a made-up topic whilst 'they' get richer.

There were times in my earlier life where I noticed that people were scared to talk to me when I was in a wheelchair, such as the usual question to my Mum or carer of, "Does he take sugar in his tea?" rather than to asking me directly. I was also mistaken constantly as another lad in school who was wheelchair-bound, so people seemed to look at the chair rather than the lad in it.

The most embarrassing part, though, is farting or, worse, following through, if you get my meaning; I barely have any muscles in my bottom. Now, picture me using crutches while going around in a shop, and the sales assistant would ask about any help. We would discuss what I want to buy but, suddenly, a twist in my stomach occurs and that means wind. Now, it is the worst kind if a full English breakfast was eaten beforehand. I would already know what the consequences were going to be. I would try to hold it in as long as possible with a bead of sweat running down my cheek, either facially or bum cheeks. Now, the difficult part comes and it is to march up to the tills to buy the said products, then there would be an echo sound as my legs landed on the floor. In an attempt to disguise the sounds more so, a large cough occurs, but it's obvious what is going on and a mass evacuation of the shop is next followed by me hurrying out. I would then cross out that shop on my list out of a fear of embarrassment if the same chap would recognise me again.

The next thing is as confusing as anything to me; why do non-disabled people park in disabled bays outside shops? The mystery is that I cannot be in their shoes nor can 'normal' people be in mine. I often wonder how difficult it is for them to walk. It must be, as so many people park in the bays to avoid walking ten more metres down into the usual car park spaces. They maybe give themselves the excuse that they are only going to be ten minutes, or that they won't cause too much hassle, as to maybe justify things. Maybe they think, what is a disability anyway? "I've got a painful bunion on my foot and that would be classed as a disability, wouldn't it?" So, it's really annoying for me, and a lot of other disabled folks, as I have had a fair few people approach me as I just finish parking my car in a disabled space. The people would see me as a young chap, put two and two together to make five, and be ready to give me a mouthful. It is only when they see the crutches on the passenger seat that they say, "Oops, I thought you were going to be a naughty guy, but I can see you need the space".

On another point, I reflected on how many of those plastic garden seats I have demolished in my life. It has got to be near enough five or six of them. The same with toilet seats which I have broken. Now, I am pants at Maths but my simple equation on this subject goes like this; my body mass + angled right hip + momentum = broken seat and bruised arse. I have a lot of ailments, which is true, but these make up in my very fast reflexes as I am a professional at falling over. It's like time slows down as I get my hands ready to take the impact. In fact, I have such great reflexes that I would have been a good fielder for England's cricketers, but the bump on the head at school made me shy away from the sport! However, even with my quick reactions, nothing can help when the snap of the plastic garden chair goes off and I am like an upside-down turtle trying to get back up.

Whenever I get an invite to a fancy dress party, it would either get thrown in the bin as if it never arrived or I would politely say that I was booked to be somewhere else on that date. However, now I am married and have been invited to a few parties, so I had to change my mind about this. The thoughts crossed my mind such as, I have dark hair and I'm Italian-looking, so I could look like a mafia hitman, but how many hitmen have walking issues? This means that the real variation is to stick to the nearest body shape I have, and to portray Quasimodo or the Phantom of the Opera.

One time, during the run-up towards Christmas, I, Yulia, and Anya decided to go to Chatsworth House, which was organising a Russian-themed Christmas. Yulia dressed up as Father Christmas's granddaughter called Snegurochka and Anya dressed up as a snowflake. Yulia mentioned in the morning prior to the visit that there was a Santa Claus costume in the wardrobe, where I politely advised it was not going to happen. However, just as we were leaving home, I looked at them both looking lovely in their costumes and suddenly had a change of heart, so I turned the car back home, which Yulia was extremely happy about. So, here was I in my Santa costume being wheeled around in my chair, along with the extravagant costumes worn by Yulia and Anya, and so we had plenty of heads turning around. However, the children were approaching me as Santa and they were telling me what they wanted for Christmas, wondering if I would be able to deliver presents in a wheelchair. I thought I was going to give children nightmares thinking Santa was not very well and that they'd be presentless (really? That word is also not in the dictionary? Come on! Yes, there is no such word as 'presentless' but I am determined to re-write the dictionary with a few more words so use them please, and together we'll get them in one day!) It almost felt like being a character from Little Britain; that man who said, "I want that one". I felt that the staff at this venue were very polite but, for sure, thought that I was 'special' in many ways. Should the beard come off and should I say, "I am normal!" but the answer is that this is a question that would be answered with another question; What is normal?

Chapter 21

Ice Cold

Ok, that's analysing having a disability done, so it gives you an insight to the daily life of what can happen. We will now analyse me and how I do things a little bit more. Now, I have been brought up to know a fair bit about golf and I'm really a secret fan of golf but, like football, it's not something I agree with; getting paid so much to move a ball from one place to the target. I keep my views to myself on this, as football seems to be life to most men and some women. However, golf seems to have a bit more class and skill to it, as you don't often see men swearing or spitting on the course or see them arguing with stewards like footballers do with referees. So, when I hear someone talking about golf, my ears would prick up and I would have the compulsion to get involved in this conversation. I'd start off by giving my know-how on the game of golf, and then they'd ask if I play. My answer would get a laugh, as I would say I swing for the ball and would end up on my arse. Next, I would say that I grew up surrounded by golf with my Dad and Ashley, and then state how well they are both doing; My Dad being a low handicap golfer and Ashley being a professional, I would proudly say. I would then roll off all the places where Ashley worked - at Royal Mid-Surrey and Wentworth, then at Palheiro in Madeira - to boast, somewhat. I would mention the place Ashley is now and try to get them to go, telling them that I would do a nice deal for them as if I was my brother's promoter. I had a fair few drives in golf buggies, having a few close shaves when the contours of the course got rocky and the buggy nearly rolled over. When the Schumacher brother of mine decides to take the wheel, I would start praying for my life. He drives fast yet so accurately, I hate him.... Nah, I love him really.

I get grumpy so much when I cannot dress myself and think about what will happen in the years to come. Yulia often comes to my rescue when my fused right foot gets stuck in my trouser leg, or when I cannot get my pants on. However, occasionally, my stubbornness comes into play where the clean pants get thrown into the bin and I go commando on that day. I am a sucker for my time-keeping and as my pal, Dave, would say, "Northers, I can set my watch by the time you arrive" as I always arrived at the right time. Now that I am a married man with a wife, time became like a rubber which bends too often. There is a choice to be grumpy or to ring people to let them know they're going to be late. The other ploy is to tell my family that they have to be at a place by 8.15 but really it is 8.30, and therefore they would make it on time. Crafty, huh?!

My wife is a violinist and therefore a lover of classical music, however, I am totally opposite to such. There are instances where I and Anya will be in the audience when we go to support Yulia performing. Then, during the intervals, members of the audience would come up to me as they understood that I was the husband. I would, of course, state how proud I am of my wife; this being true, as she spends so many hours of rehearsing for concerts. Then, the conversation would go further about the pieces of music that were performed, where they would say how they were filled with emotion and so on. I had truly felt nothing when the classical music was played, apart from proud of my wife. I feel that it's just a whole bunch of notes, it has nothing really to latch onto, and I cannot understand how those notes depict a certain scene or an emotion. Really, though, I have no connection unless there are real visualisations going off, like how Charlie Chaplin used music to aid his films or how cartoons used music for affect. I would prefer words to help with understanding. To be frank, though, I would look at the audience when classical music is being played and try to understand what on earth they are thinking. One idea is that they are being pompous and it's like the champagne and caviar thing where you have to be seen to like it to look posh, even though it is like eating rocks of salt with a funny-tasting Alka-Seltzer. I often think it is a lot of jumping on the bandwagon to fit into the culture, but not really enjoying or believing that they enjoy such. I would prefer to go to a Rock concert and get an adrenaline rush. I had, in my single life, seen many concerts with my friends, Dave and Marky. I saw bands like Pink Floyd in Earl's Court where, only the week before, one of the audience stands had collapsed and injured so many folks. I was somewhat nervous in going, but I was sure that they would have repaired it in that time. Dave and I got to our seats and the lights went down then, the next thing, a guy right in front of us lit up what we thought was a cigarette, as you could smoke in venues at that time, but the smell was something much stronger and the smoke made Dave and I felt a bit spaced out. It made all the lasers and fireworks seem all so much better. When Sam Brown, one of Pink Floyd's backing vocalists belted out 'Great Gig in the Sky' I had goose bumps, as she is an amazing singer. I saw Meatloaf four times who, as an entertainer, has never let me down with my expectations. I saw Brian May in concert twice, but Alice Cooper was something which was entertaining but yet it was the volume that stunned Dave and I. We both got into my car afterwards and saw each other's mouths moving but heard nothing at all. A few days of recuperation enabled us to hear again.

There is the topic of sex. I was a virgin until Yulia came along, and it was in Torquay that we discovered we were right for each other in every way; mentally, emotionally, and sexually. I have no embarrassment saying I was in my 30's at the time of losing my virginity. I was in no rush, apart from a few moments of wishing whilst in my teens but, once that passed, I was waiting for the right lady in my life.

I am more unique than you know already, even though I am like any other man with usual man's bits. However, when it comes to the bedroom department I am different, as I could not climax naturally. I could only orgasm with icy cold water! HOW, did I hear you ask? Well, I will tell you. It was discovered during my puberty that, when I went swimming, it was brilliant how usual diving under water is, but I could never understand why the backstroke was invented, as you just bump into other swimmers due to not seeing them coming. I would get out of the pool and then make my way to the changing rooms, where I would have to go through a cold foot wash to prevent a verruca, but I noticed two things happening to me; my manhood got bigger, and a strange liquid came out from it but it sure was not urine. It was nothing that I wanted to discuss with anyone but, when I got to know what sex was all about from watching certain films, I knew it was sperm. This is where I realised that I could orgasm by having icy cold water on my foot but, later, I found out that it was the ONLY way. You're probably wondering why I am sharing such intimate details with you. If I was in my twenties, I would not have divulged it, but now I am in my forties and I want to break barriers as I think being open can help others. There was an interesting moment in my life in Amsterdam when I travelled with Marky and a group of friends. We landed from a short flight but, after we had landed, the plane rolled on for what seemed like another hour until it reached the terminal. From the airport, we took a van taxi and had a competition to see the first attractive lady in a window with a red light on. This was funny because the first chap shouted, 'There's one!' but, as we got nearer, there was a bulge in the lady's knickers which suggested she was more than a lady, so this chap got picked on for most of the holiday together. Regularly, we would see a lady in the window and it would be questioned of whether we were sure it was a lady! Now, this holiday was pre-Yulia, and it was in this stage in my life where I thought I was going to be single forever and wouldn't experience sex. So, I brought extra money and thought I would participate in the legal sex trade. As I walked with Marky, with every street looking the same as there were no landmarks apart from a canal, I spotted one lady; Spanish-looking, and definitely only a woman. This woman smiled at me with interest (some women saw me with my legs and gave an indication that they were not up for the challenge) so I thought to go in. Now, I first thought I wanted to have sex but later, did not. I thought, firstly, it was a dangerous thing even with protection, and secondly, I wanted to have sex with someone I really connected with. So, the other variation was that the lady would please me by using her hands. Without a word of me speaking about my need for cold water and ejaculation problems, she would change hands every five minutes or so until fifteen minutes had gone. She asked for another fifteen minutes to be paid if I wished to continue; of course, I was enjoying and paid up. Thirty minutes later, she gave up the challenge, and said sorry that she could not make me climax and that it had never happened to her before. I had a compulsion to tell her about the cold water thing so that she did not feel bad but it was a lovely thirty minutes in my life, for which I thanked her for, although it was a stressful thirty minutes for the lady and my nether region was aching for a good few days after. My group of friends all cheered after I came out from this long session, and they thought I was 'The Man' as she kissed me for all to see on the lips to say goodbye.

I also experienced a certain cake in Amsterdam and smoked a certain relaxing 'cigarette', which had more than tobacco, purchased in a cafe. It was relaxing me, for sure, but I was still aware of my surroundings. To be frank, it was better than alcohol for two reasons; the first being that I could still walk and secondly, my leg pains vanished for days afterwards. However, the combination of a lot of alcohol and the cake made me not so good on my feet, where one moment of lost balance as crutches slipped on rainy paving stones bought me one step away from diving into a canal. So, I kept away from the alcohol for a few days afterwards. After smoking this substance, I actually realised that I had pains in my legs but was ignorant to it, as I felt wonderful for the first few days. Even though it was good for me medically, I did not want to do anything illegally in England so I just put the whole Amsterdam experience as a great adult memory and shared it amongst others rarely... Until now! Later in my life, I have questioned in my head why marijuana is illegal in the UK but is ok in other countries. The great things about it are the medical help it gives, it does not give a hangover, and it does not make people aggressive, in fact, it does the opposite and makes people calm and happy. Research proves that more people die from alcohol and tobacco-related illnesses; compare that to marijuana, which has probably not killed anyone. Personally, I would ban alcohol and cigarettes and introduce marijuana. I have also learned that marijuana helps towards improving, or cures, cancers.

Marky and I, plus our other pals, returned to Amsterdam a year later to see in the New Year. Now, I never liked New Year celebrations. It was like waiting for the clock to chime 12, and then people go crazy. For me, I could not get it. Firstly, it was just to annoy the sleep pattern, as I would prefer an earlier night, and secondly, it's usually in a venue with a lot of drunk people, loud music, and just basically claustrophobic. In a few words, I did not enjoy this event. So, in the hotel where we stayed was a lovely bar, and I knew that a pub crawl was going to happen as it usually did when going out. I waved off the group of lads, including Marky, and proceeded to go to the bar. I asked for a double brandy and, since I was only guy at the bar with the stewardess, we struck up a conversation. More double brandies kept coming and more conversation. It was nearing 11pm and, by this time, the brandies were working very well and I therefore struggled to speak, but the stewardess and I had already swapped contact details. We have actually kept in contact with each other since. There may have been some chemistry between us, but I never took it further. It was dampened very quickly as the lads returned because they felt they could not let one of the lads, meaning me, see in the New Year alone. I was drunklingly (yes, I know it is not word in the dictionary!) annoyed on their early arrival, thus interrupting the conversation between the two of us, and it was then noted by the lads about these two 'love birds', so I thought it was a good enough time to go to my room. It was nice to see her via Facebook getting married and having a baby during 2013 for me and I suppose it would have been the same for her to see me getting married in 2008.

Anyway, more about the trip to Amsterdam! The guy in the group who loved to pub crawl also wanted to see a certain sex museum. It apparently showed the porn industry throughout the ages. Armed with a map, off the lads and I went. Each road looked the same - canal then a street - so it was easy to get lost. The lads did lose track so much and, me with my crutches slowed the group down, but, eventually, we got into this iconic museum. I found the nearest seat after this fifteen minute walk and there I stayed, whilst the rest of the group looked around. Amsterdam was a place that had sex everywhere. It was not like you had to walk for what seemed hours just to see that museum; there were others looking very similar and not so far away, so I was wishing annoyingly that I had a voodoo doll of this mate in our group to change his views on where to go. It was the same when Marky had his stag do in Blackpool, the same guy wanted to pub crawl but it could not be to the next nearest pub, it had to be another ten minutes' walk to be the one he wanted... Boy, I would have given him my mind if I had the balls to say about it. On the upside of that stag do, I was the only chap in the group who 'pulled', as this young lady made a beeline towards me. Before we knew it, we were making out in the bar. Now, if I saw a couple doing such, I would say to myself, "Find a hotel room" but really, it's a free country, and why waste the chance that was offered to me, as you know these things happened so seldom? This lady and I had just swapped mobile numbers when the pub crawler of the group said it was time to move on, more's the pity. However, when I got up it must have been a shock, as I tried to make arrangements via mobile phone to meet up later but it never happened.

So, let's get back to the subject of sex and icy cold water. See, I told you I go off in tangents and it would not be so good being half-drunk whilst reading this! I introduced the issues carefully to Yulia after we had sex for the first time, as she wanted to know if I climaxed. Now, I thought that this could make things hard for Yulia to comprehend and may actually be grounds to separate as I was not fulfilling Yulia possibly, however, she was fine about it completely. The only problem was that it was difficult to plan, as both of us would get in the mood whilst hugging and kissing but then have to stop to get a bowl of cold water. It kind of ruined the moment, plus we did not want our daughter to wake up from the commotion only to ask why Mum had a bowl of water. "Well, Dad's feet stink and I am going to wash them" was the quickest explanation. The cold water issue was not popular unless we wanted to try for a baby, which Yulia and I did try and, to this day, we would love to have a baby together. At one point of us trying for two years together, we thought that something must not be right, so I went to have a sperm test. On the day of the test, I rang them up and asked, strangely enough, for a bowl of icy cold water. The lady who took that phone call was confuddled, but she said that she would sort that out. I came to the reception and asked if the cold water was ready and, surely enough, it was. I was shown into the room where there was a choice of either erotic magazines or DVDs, but it was over within seconds of my foot diving into the bowl. The receptionist had a shocked expression as I came out so fast, and she said that men are usually there for a good fifteen minutes! The test proved that my sperm were swimming very healthily inside me, so Yulia had some checks where it was proven that fibroids were in her womb, which had to be taken out.

Yulia was in hospital for the operation, and when I came to

visit with Anya it was a shock to see her still coming around from the anaesthetic, barely being able to talk. It was all too much. I broke down in tears as I could not hold them back anymore, and this snowballed onto Anya. We both wanted to take her home to look after her but, of course, it was not possible. It was better the next day when Yulia texted me to say how she was feeling and, on visiting, it was more positive and the operation was a success. Yulia came out after three days of hospital and she recovered at home successfully, much to mine and Anya's joy.

Chapter 22

I Do Deserve This

As I mentioned to you already, I was at the most happiest with having a wife and daughter at my side. However, there are days that I cannot believe where I am and I wonder whether I deserve to be in that place. It's like the words of the bullies eating away at me, saying, "You're not good enough!" Even to this date, I sometime have that one moment and say to myself that I am not good enough; it's like the story from 'The Phantom of the Opera'. I watched the Andrew Lloyd Webber's production three times and every time it tugs at my heart strings. This is purely for the fact that he could not experience love and a man who was 'more' perfect, Raoul, wins Christine's heart. Yes, the phantom felt he could not fit in as he was persecuted and bullied for looking odd, so he hid away and became aggressive, as he had no real connection with other people. I related to this so very much, in the sense of wanting to hide away, and that I wanted no bad attention drawn to me. I felt that I could never win the heart of a young lady, looking how I did. Upon having the love of Yulia, I just cannot believe it or think I deserve it. It also amazes some people to see Yulia and I. I have very good intuition and, when people see me with Yulia for the first time, they are thinking, why is such a beautiful lady with this freak? They may think things like I and Yulia met via a Russian website and that the relationship is based on a lie. They don't see how hard we work together, and how much affection there is at home with each other. Sure, there are bad days which every couple gets and we have decided that a shouting match at each other is not the way to go so we talk out any issues. We said, from the start, that we wanted to be an open book with each other and that is what happens. In regards to my personality, I have a big urge to be liked. It derives from the time of being bullied at school and I really wanted to fit in so, by being nice, it kind of helped me to fit in. All the time, when I am out in a public area, I smile at strangers and, if someone smiles back, I feel like I have made connection. The same goes for when I am at work; I treat customers the way I want to be treated so, if I get that same level back, it feels like a lovely sense of connection that can bring happy tears. Yet, being nice to others was the total opposite to how I treated myself, as you know by the self-harm and the drinking.

There is still one problem though and that's that I drink alcohol still, which is not good in many ways, like it's not good for the family or my health. Again, alcohol numbs the senses but it doesn't drive them away forever as they do come back. It's annoying to me that I have a dependency on alcohol still, and not to live in the pain and work it out more. As I also mentioned previously, I believe marijuana is better replacement to alcohol. In fact, I decided to write about, and explore, why I still drink. I thought that getting married and being a Dad would be a huge tick on my list of things to do in my life. Yet there is still a feeling of void in my life, and that's being able to love myself still. I think that the hatred that I had forced upon me at such an impressionable age of my school years, not being able to connect with other children, the feeling of being isolated, and not being accepted as attractive lad in my early teens, have made up a confused mind. This has made it difficult to love myself; sometimes I still feel isolated and sometimes I crave for isolation. I love my family dearly and would not change anything of that style of life. It's just that I dealt with a huge chunk of my life by myself (supported, of course, by my parents) and I felt that that was how it was meant to be, where my motto was; "People like me are to be single forever, who wants a defective person in their lives?" So, I feel lucky to have my wife and daughter around me but feel sometimes non-deserving and that makes a bit of a battle in my mind and values still.

Subconsciously, I sometimes try to make my wife grumpy at me, so that it would be just enough to make her leave as then it would give me the same feelings of, "See, I told you you weren't good enough!" That's a huge part of my destructive side; the feeling of not being good enough. I would start many projects, look at them, and say they were not good enough, so I never accomplished many things on that basis. Maybe it is because I like the sense of being away from the physical pain that I experience, hence why I want to be out by drink. Maybe I just like the taste of it, as a Tequila Sunrise or a White Russian is very nice indeed, but not quite because I have to get to the point where I feel drunk. Maybe it's the punishment aspect really that is true. Alcohol is like a punch to the head, and takes away the emotional pain. It's buried deeply into my psychology that I do not deserve to fit into society, and that was only from experiences in my childhood. These pains never go away with however much of drinking, counselling, or how much love Yulia gives to me. It's just one thing that cannot change unless I want it. But do I want it? Does it do anything for me to keep this pain and let it come out every now and then?

Alcohol only gives a sore head in the mornings and regret as an emotion. I have then, throughout the day, pains in my gut and bad stomachs. I have already had my fair share of alcohol in my thirties, so I had lessened the amount and avoided hard spirits, like vodka or rum. However, this is not a good example for my daughter, plus Yulia misses out on me being my usual self. So, it's an event that is no good for anybody concerned who loves me. How do I get out of this pain that is not hurting me or anybody around me? That is one good question. Talking helps me very much; it takes the edge off the pain, but still it comes back. Hugs and kisses from Yulia calm me down and are extremely appreciated, yet the bad stuff comes back. So, this negativity, how does it help me? It helps because I am who I am. I am not ego-driven, I am shy, I'm not so confident, and I'm happy all the time to those who see me at work or on the street. It's the English way, I guess. "I'm alright", but how many are really not and it's like the swan idea; looking graceful on top of the water yet legs going so fast to make it look good. So, if I did not have those emotional and physical scars, would I be the opposite and therefore not as so endearing, who knows? I thought that maybe I should get a punch bag to get out the stress that I sometimes feel but, again, that's short-term. Unfortunately, there is no easy path in life; we are who we are and, looking back on the near-death experience, I learnt that we are here to learn. What it is that we are learning is unclear, as I had this experience at a young age, and it is like a distant memory to me now. However, I know that what I saw in the future helped me to change my adult life for the better. The biggest thing I have learnt is to be kind to myself as, no matter how much love Yulia, Anya, or my parents can give or show, it has to come from within. It has to be the words in my mind of, "actually, I am alright", "I have done the best I could", and "I do deserve this". This realisation warms my heart and brings a tear or two to my eyes as I am writing, and a lot of pain has flown away. I will try to remember these words and do my best to let them sink in. However, I continue to drink and think as to why. I am adamant that I want to escape myself still; I just don't like how I look. It's a medicine to knock me out, as sometimes I am tired of the physical pains too, with most things I take still not giving me a deep sleep. Even though I know my wife loves me for who I am, I still suffer with my own acceptance.

Conclusion

Now, to conclude the story, it only ends my life up to now which is in my very early forties - forty three, to be precise. Sadly, Mr Newton, my surgeon from my childhood, died from asbestosis as he worked on a boiler which had asbestos. Along with my parents, I wrote a thankful and caring article in the Derby Evening Telegraph to celebrate Mr Newton's life, as I would not be the man I am today without all of his skill.

Yulia and I have celebrated seven years of marriage, which surprised some people in England and some in Russia, as there were comments of, "Give it a year". Yulia's orchestra in Tula kept her place for just over a year, in case she came back. I have still not learnt Russian to a very good standard, but can understand it more than to speak it, which helps when Yulia and Anya talk in Russian as to not let Anya forget her first language. However, I envisioned myself in later life living out in Russia; perhaps I would get to know Russian but then forget English. Yet, Yulia has settled in well into the English style of life, so when she does go back over to see family and friends, she struggles with the Russian culture. There is very little customer service in supermarkets, for example, as the staff all have a grumpy expression. Also, there's the fact that the drivers never acknowledge if they are allowing the other driver to go first. Actually no, there is no allowing of any kind; it's who has the biggest balls to avoid the head-on crash. I love to drive, but it would be no chance at all that I would drive in Russia as it is like a bumper car ride and especially worse when on long stretchy roads which has numerous potholes.

I had bad news in the last six years of my Dad having prostate cancer, which then developed into terminal cancer. This was a huge shock in my world as I had that news whilst at work and I could not do anything, so I was sent home by my manager. I dived into the arms of Yulia and that eased the pain while I cried the hurt out. Yet, with treatment and motivation, my Dad is still doing very well and regularly going out to fish or play golf. Plus, my parents are often going on cruise ships to beautiful places and seeing Ashley with my family in Spain.

Still I cannot believe it, sometimes, that I am married and a Dad to such a lovely daughter; there are no ifs or buts about being a Step-Dad, as I am just Dad. As for being a husband; just to wake up next to the lady that I love means more than anything in the world to me. Even if a bad day ever happened, I just get a hug from Yulia and it makes everything right. However, I still thought about the 'what ifs' in my life, like if I had normal legs and was not bullied. Would I end up being a sports-mad man kicking balls (pardon the pun) everywhere and I would end up being ego-driven, not the kind, shy, and lacking in confidence, which really is not a bad quality at all?

There are a few more things that I dream of. Firstly, to be possible to be a Dad the second time around. If that happens naturally then it will, or a bowl of cold water will do! Anya would love a sister so that she can share things with her and, really, Yulia and I had been trying so much but we are not there just yet. I wonder about how fast those forty years had gone already and how long I have left on the planet, although not in a negative way, as I have no concerns since my near-death experience. It was almost like I was wishing life away when I was single, but now the opposite is true since Yulia and Anya came into my life. When my life is over, I would like it not to be upsetting, so I would like to be carried into a venue, not necessarily a church, with the Benny Hill theme tune. On the way out, it would be 'Manamana.' In my own thoughts, it should not be that expensive to have someone buried and it should be a celebration of that person's life. It's just my wish or thoughts.

I had done other things, like having my head shaved for the Swap Tears for Smiles charity and raised over £300. I was very proud as it started as a joke at my workplace but, when I started to ask for donations for this act, there was no going back. The shave was done at work by one of my colleagues and, within half an hour, I was completely bald. I dived into the men's bathroom to see the result and it was this thug looking straight back at me in the mirror. It was the same reaction for Yulia and Anya, who thought they had an escaped convict in their midst. I began to change my eating habits, since the ulcer scare. I cut out wheat, potatoes, fruits, and dairy products as much as possible. It was inspired by The Stone Age diet which I found on a certain website. The diet has been proven for me as I am a lot slimmer and still enjoy food. I learnt so much more from the website such as about fluoride and how damaging it is to health, so I try to let other folks know. It is a myth that fluoride cleans teeth and, in fact, it was used by Nazis in concentration camps to make the prisoners docile.

I still dream of walking much better than I do to today. I am not concerned in regards to the risks of it all, but more to the money side of things, as taking time off work would mean a reduced income. The operations would have to work on every joint, from ankles to knees to hips, so it would mean a lot of recuperation. I am in the happiest of times of my life, but I still would like to walk better, as walking with convex knees is tiring and getting worse with arthritis. In fact, my knees are more bent than ever before and making it extremely difficult to mobilise myself. Sadly, just to walk a few meters is quite painful and tiresome, meaning that crutches are used more so. It does not help with the fact that I was diagnosed with minor bone disease of the spine, so it's one more ailment to add to the list. My thoughts regarding my body are now to laugh about it, rather than something else.

I hope, by now, that you feel that I am quite level-headed and, just briefly before the book ends, I would like to tell you my recent interest and wish for the world/society. I have interest in all things in life like UFO's, where I constantly look out for new sightings or documentaries. I wonder that, in my lifetime, will there be the awakening that all people will know we are not alone in the universe. Let us go back to my near-death experience and life review, which suggested that we are ALL part of each other so it's imbedded in me that I have feelings of not being alone. We are one consciousness making different memories.

In fact, Yulia, Anya, and I all saw a UFO when we were driving home. Anya spotted it first but I was not too sure until we pulled over outside our home. It was difficult to see as it was night-time, but there was an orb of light that just stayed in the sky. It seemed to revolve around like a glowing bright yellow light ball and flashes of red. It stayed visible for a minute or so but then whoosh, it went straight up into the night's sky at lightning speed. That began to spiral my interest, as I had always felt that we are not alone in the universe. Plus, discussing the incident with my parents sparked their memories of seeing a huge UFO a few decades before.

More so than this, I really feel like I have woken up somewhat in my consciousness. I had my thirties where I cannot remember so much, apart from where things began to improve when it was understood Yulia loved me and the drinking of alcohol lessened. I have improved so much more on this, but not totally, as I still have this destructive nature that I still want to improve, and one day I will get there.

I reflect so much more on the near-death experience in my forties that I did in my teens, and how it manifested itself to where I am now. I believe that we are all connected together and that we are here on earth to learn from, and love, one another. I feel, sometimes, that my thoughts are something that are fed into me and especially what the general public would term as conspiracy theories. It becomes less theoretical, though, when evidence comes into existence, therefore making it proof. There are forces that are stopping us from being who we really are, and stopping us from being free. To paraphrase the late great George Carlin, we have really two main political parties, like red vs blue. Whoever wins on the election day reverts their statements and do what they want, but it gives the public a sense of being free in a democracy. We have those two choices as the other smaller groups get nowhere in popularity, yet we have hundreds of different flavoured ice-creams, don't we?

There are those who want the human population to lessen so there will be more for the few dominating. Just to give a few clues, research the Georgia Guidestones and maybe take a minute to watch Bill Gates on the Ted Talk, where he blatantly said, in summary, that he wanted to reduce the population. Oh, and the Queen's other half is famously quoted to say that, in his next reincarnation, he wanted to be a deadly virus to reduce the population; you may wonder why I am not a royalist. They, whoever they are, want to dumb down the majority on earth so that we are more docile and easier to control. There are more rules and legislation to follow to take away people's control.

David Icke and Jim Marrs (both worth researching, amongst many others) has given me a huge amount of awareness to this all and, basically, opened my mind to all these possibilities. I really feel that it is time for a lot of us to have a bigger insight into our reality that we see, as there is more than meets the eye. There are the few - the ones who are in power - who are controlling the TV screens, putting stuff on for children to make them more docile, less focused, behave worse (so they get sedated), and to follow like sheep. People need to be made aware that there is symbolism in so much film/music, plus demon rituals performed on stage from famous singers are done purposely so that it become natural for humanity to be immune, and this controls more so. Things like chemtrails are getting noted more so, and may keep doing so.

There is a much bigger picture, and it is ok to have fun and enjoy life as that's what makes us human. Yet, we need to keep our eye on the ball and to be free from a cage. We need to question everything and stick together, challenging what we think is wrong – not to go along with what the rules and regulations are, as 'they' stop us from being us and being free. There is more to life than work, sleep, buy, and then retire - if we are lucky to retire and be in good health to do the things we have dreamt of doing. Yet, we vote the political parties in to look after us, and they change the retirement age so most of 'us' get even more older and less able to do things. Things are not going in the right direction and I am not inciting violence, as you may realise that that's not what I am. I am inciting non-compliance in the rules/laws that if you feel are wrong, they usually are. I don't believe protests work either; it's a ploy to get folks to feel able to join together but then nothing much comes from it, but maybe I am wrong.

I am not, and never will be, a racist, sexist, or any ist apart from a togetherist; yes, another word made up by yours truly. The things that separate have been designed for one reason alone; to divide and conquer. Whilst most of the public argue over these differences, the bankers are quietly taking our money. Yes, they designed a thing called money and, they make us, the public, poor by having low incomes and high interest rates, so we'll never pay things back, and the banks that loan the money never had the money in the first place. They simply transfer that amount onto your account, and then you spend most of your life paying it back, plus interest.

One last thing that I urge folks to do is to investigate certain events of 9/11, which was orchestrated, for sure, but not how the media portrayed it. Please see for yourself the things I have come across, and I'll make the list of 12 facts below:

1. Building 7 came down on the same day as the Twin Towers, but this building was not hit by any planes. Most buildings don't just come down from a fire; they usually become a burned-out shell of a building.

2. Building 7 was reported, by a BBC reporter on live TV, as a building that had just collapsed, even though it was standing completely fine in the background. Therefore, there are scripts that the presenters must follow.

3. The owner of these buildings took out a different insurance policy, where he would gain more money in the unlikely event of a plane hitting a building he owned. It was a double pay-out if it was two buildings.

4. The owner of these buildings had his breakfast daily on the top floor of one of the Twin Towers, but he did not on that day.

5. No black boxes were found, anywhere, from the Twin Towers, the Pentagon, and Flight 93. Yet, they managed to find a passport of a terrorist; amazing, huh?

6. You would have thought that Bin Laden would have been proud, and boasted that he committed this act. He denied it strongly. Also, all planes were grounded right after 9/11, yet 'they' flew Bin Laden's family out from the USA.

7. There was a training exercise, on that day, of terrorists taking over planes, so it confused staff involved as to what was real and what was a 'training exercise'. Funnily enough, there was a training exercise during the 7/7 attack in London, too; the training was being held at the exact same

stations where the terrorists were at the same time. I would be laughing, but we are talking about lives taken from our humankind, our relatives.

8. Phone calls were made from victims in the plane during the hijack. The height and speed of the planes would have made this impossible, so this needs further investigation.

9. The Pentagon was attacked on the same part where an on-going investigation was being made due to money missing from the Pentagon's budget. The day before 9/11 happened, it was announced that billions were missing that could not be answered for.

10. There was no clear CCTV footage of a plane hitting the Pentagon, the most secure building ever, you would have thought. All we, the public, saw were stills from a camera, but this evidently does not show a plane.

11. No large debris of planes were found from any of the crashes.

12. How is it possible that aluminium wings and tail pieces of the planes were able to cut through buildings? It would be to my poor education, but this light metal cannot cut through steel surely.

I could make a longer list, although I will draw your attention to Dr Judy Woods and Andrew Johnson's research, as it will be worth your time.

I dream of being free from work but still making myself busy in playing and composing music or writing more books. However, the biggest thing I want is for people to get along. Communication and understanding is the key.

Maybe if this book is successful, I may write Part Two later in my life.

Thank you for reading, and I hope you enjoyed reading some of the things that have happened to me. Most of all, I hope it has helped you somewhat, as that was my aim.

Self-Publishing Your Book Made Easy!

Sazmick Books, offer self-publishing, editing and marketing services to authors of most genres. We help to fulfill your ambition of getting your work from typed or written manuscript, into a printed book or E-book with customisable add-ons.

Simple packages, Stunning books.

Chat with us and get your book on the road today!

www.sazmickbooks.com

For All Your Self-Publishing Needs